Benjamin Franklin King

Ben King's Verse

Benjamin Franklin King

Ben King's Verse

ISBN/EAN: 9783337028695

Printed in Europe, USA, Canada, Australia, Japan

Cover: Foto ©Thomas Meinert / pixelio.de

More available books at **www.hansebooks.com**

Ben King's Verse

BEN KING'S VERSE

EDITED BY NIXON WATERMAN
INTRODUCTION BY JOHN McGOVERN
BIOGRAPHY BY OPIE READ

CHICAGO
FORBES &
COMPANY
1899

COPYRIGHT, 1894, 1898
BY ASENETH BELL KING

BEN KING'S VERSE
SECOND EDITION, WITH ADDITIONS

FIRST PRINTING, AUGUST, 1898
SECOND PRINTING, NOVEMBER, 1898
THIRD PRINTING, APRIL, 1899
COMPLETING FIFTH THOUSAND

THE DRAWINGS IN THIS VOLUME ARE CONTRIBUTED BY CHAS. A. GRAY, W. W. DENSLOW, H. G. MARATTA, RAY BROWN, F. HOLME, J. T. MCCUTCHEON, HORACE TAYLOR, WM. SCHMEDTGEN, T. E. POWERS, AND HARRY O. LANDERS. COVER AND TITLE PAGE DESIGNED BY HOWARD BOWEN.

INTRODUCTION

SO FAR as we know, this young man, now so suddenly dead, was the drollest mimic and gentlest humorist of our region. He existed as the welcome and mirthful shadow of conventional and tiresome things.

He began as the expositor of "The Maiden's Prayer" on the piano, where each accented note was flat or sharp, and the music flowed rapidly, or over great difficulties, as the score might determine. He arose, and looking half-witted, recited with unapproachable modesty the stammering delight which he would feel "if he could be by Her!" He frowsled his hair and became Paderewski, who forthwith fell upon the piano tooth and nail, tore up the track, derailed the symphony, went down stairs and shook the furnace, fainted at the pedals, and was carried out rigid by supers—the greatest pianist of any age. He wrote "If I Should Die To-night"—a parody that was accepted as the true original, the sun, the center of the

Introduction

great If-I-should-die-to-night system of thought and poetry. He wrote the poet's lament—that there was nothing to eat but food, and nowhere to come but off. The artists of the newspaper world generously sprang to his side; they placed him pictorially before the people, and determined, with almost prophetic spirit, that our small circle should not alone dwell with undiminishing laughter upon the gambols of Ben King. He was coldly, then not coldly, then warmly received by the church fairs, the clubs, and the Elks, where he got a supper—if any were left. At last he charged a small sum for appearing publicly, and this sum was rapidly enlarging and his fortune was in sight, when the hotel porter found him dead in his room at Bowling Green, Kentucky.

During the years we knew him, he never spoke to us in a disparaging way concerning any other person, and unless Paderewski's comb was ruffled by Ben's exhibition of hair and haste in piano-playing, no parody, or perk, or prank of Ben King ever depended for its success upon the wounding of another creature's feelings.

We all accounted him a genius, and while we could not guess what he would do next, we awaited his performances with complacence, laughing as if we

Introduction

owned him and had ourselves ordered his latest *jeu d' esprit.*

We deplored the untimely moment of his end; we held beautiful, solemn and impressive memorial services over his body, with music by the sweet singers whom he had loved when he was alive, and touching words by ministers of the gospel; we buried him affectionately, as one who could least be spared from our circle; and as we were the witnesses of what he did, we now charge ourselves to be the testimonies of his rare talents. JOHN MCGOVERN.

BIOGRAPHY

BENJAMIN FRANKLIN KING, JR., was born at St. Joseph, Michigan, March 17, 1857, and died at Bowling Green, Kentucky, April 7, 1894. He was married Nov. 27, 1883, to Aseneth Belle Latham, of St. Joseph, Michigan, by Professor David Swing at his residence in Chicago. The wife and two sons, Bennett Latham King and Spencer P. King, survive him.

While yet a child, music came to Ben King as an inspiration. His infant fingers touched the keys of a piano and a ripple of notes, strange and sweet, startled his parents into the consciousness that a great talent had been given unto him. How odd a boy he was—no one understood him. On the edge of the marsh he would sit during hours at a time, under the spell of the weird music amid the rushes. As he grew up, lacking the instincts that make men successful in business, he was pronounced a failure—not by those who had warmed themselves in the glow of his poetic

Biography

nature, but by the man who believed that to turn over a dime and thereby to make a dollar of it was the most gracious faculty that could be bestowed upon a member of the human family. But when Ben King died, St. Joseph became more widely known in one day than hundreds of excursions and a thousand orchards had served to advertise it in the past. On that April morning, people living in the far East and the far West asked the question: "Where is St. Joseph?"

Ben King was not only a man of music; he was a poet, a gentle satirist, and a humorist of the highest order. Every company was brightened by his coming, every man felt better for having heard his quaint remarks. There was about him a droll, a charming irresponsibility—a Thomas Hood from Michigan.

I find, as I have found for the fiftieth time while striving to write these lines, that I am still too much under the shock caused by his death to write dispassionately of him. My judgment, the common sense that one should bring to bear upon such a subject, is obscured by the vivid picture of an early morning; and down a dark hallway I still hear a violent knocking—and then comes a throbbing silence, and out of that silence comes an excited whisper—"Ben King is dead." OPIE READ.

CONTENTS

	PAGE
After Weidenfeller Goes	191
Angeliny	157
Appearances	94
Asphodel	29
Baby Up at Battenberg's	40
Benton Harbor, Mich	25
Beulah Land	163
Biography	ix
Blackbird and the Thrush, The	165
Bung Town Canal	184
But Then	178
Casual Observation, A	72
Cat O' Nine Tails, The	125
'Cause It's Gittin' Spring	202
Chautauquan Maid, The	62
Cleopatra and Charmian	175
Comin' Christmas Morn	233
Coonie In De Holler	189
Cow Slips Away, The	272

Contents

Cultured Girl Again, The	211
Day and The Shingle, The	262
De Blackbird Fetch De Spring	91
De Bugle On De Hill	56
De Circus Turkey	130
De Clouds Am Gwine Ter Pass	102
De Cushville Hop	213
De Eyarfquake	159
De Good Ship	71
De Massa	187
De Ribber Ob Life	122
De Spring-House	167
De Sun's Comin' Back	34
De Watah Mellen Sploshun	267
Decorate De Cabin	204
Didn't We, Jim?	147
Down in Walhallalah	248
Down the Mississippi	85
Dreamy Days	208
Ec-a-lec-tic Fits	152
Elopement	13
Evolution	5
Fates, The	45
Flower's Ball, The	30
Frog's Thanksgiving, A	113

Contents

Gedder In Yo' Grain	8
Girl With the Jersey, The	95
Gittin' My Soul Inter Shape	3
Gord Only Knows	215
Grave Matters	231
Hair-Tonic Bottle, The	128
Hank Spink	115
Heart of Hearts	254
Her Folks An' Hiz'n	17
How Hank Died	22
How Often	24
Huccum it so?	265
I Fed the Fishes	108
If I Can Be by Her	50
If I Should Die	1
If My Wife Taught School	96
I'm a Bluejay	65
Injun Summah	200
Introduction	vi
Jane Jones	10
Jes' Take My Advice	217
Keep Him a Baby	155
Lef' de Ole Hoss Out	150
Legend of the St. Joseph	240
Like De Ole Mule Bes'	119

Contents

Like the New Friends Best	73
Little Jude	244
Little Pucken Singer	246
Little 'Rasmus	78
Lovey-Loves	114
Mary Had a Cactus Plant	261
Mermaid, The	89
Miss Bahtholamew	270
Negro Song of Home, A	75
Nile, The	117
Nobody Knows	80
No Harm Done	41
Old Musician's Fate, The	220
Old Spinning Wheel, The	98
Old St. Joe	58
Ole Bossie Cow	111
Owl and the Crow, The	100
Paraphrase	47
Patriotism and a Pension	218
Pessimist, The	225
Pinkey	180
Post-Driver, The	149
Presque Isle	161
'Rastus King	67
Record F'om 'Way Back, A	227

Contents

Retrospection, A	196
River St. Joe, The	36
Sad Fate of Yim Yonson	237
Santa's Presents Fo' De Good	250
Say When, and Say It	2
She Does not Hear	83
Sofie Jakobowski	133
S'posin'	77
St. Patrick's Day	198
Summer's Afternoon, A	104
Sunrise	144
Sycamore	255
Thanksgibbin' in Ole Virginny	229
That Cat	112
That Valentine	70
Tramp, The	61
Toboggan	54
Ultimatum ,The	206
Under Obligations	171
Vi Viguers	273
Volapuk	259
When the Stage Gits In	209
Woodticks, The	145
Yaller Jackets' Nest, The	20
Zaccheus	193

IF I SHOULD DIE

IF I should die to-night
    And you should come to my cold corpse and say,
    Weeping and heartsick o'er my lifeless clay—
    If I should die to-night,
And you should come in deepest grief and woe—
And say: "Here's that ten dollars that I owe,"
    I might arise in my large white cravat
    And say, "What's that?"

    If I should die to-night
And you should come to my cold corpse and kneel,
Clasping my bier to show the grief you feel,
    I say, if I should die to-night
And you should come to me, and there and then
Just even hint 'bout payin' me that ten,
    I might arise the while,
    But I'd drop dead again.

SAY WHEN, AND SAY IT

WRITE me a poem that has n't been writ,
  Sing me a song that has n't been sung yet,
String out a strain that has n't been strung,
  And ring me a chime that has n't been rung yet.

Paint me a picture but leave out the paint,
  Pile up a pile of old scenes of my schoolery,
Leave me alone; I would fain meditate
  And mourn o'er the moments I lost in tomfoolery.

Tell me a tale that dropped out of a star,
  Push me a pun that is pungent, not earthy.
I must have something sharp, strident, and strong
  To eke out a laugh or be moderately mirthy.

Give me a love that has never been loved,
  Not knowing the glance of the bold and unwary,
A cherub abreast with the saints up above,
  And I'll get along and be passably merry.

But come on the fly to me, come on the jump,
  Do n't hang around on the outskirts and walk to me;
Throw out your chest well, and hold up your head;
  Say when, and *say* it, or else do n't you talk to me.

GITTIN' INTER SHAPE

RECKON de angel what rolled 'way de stone,
   An' let de good shepherd escape,
Some day 'll fly down to dis prison ob sin
An' lib'rate all dat's prepahed to come in;
   So I 'se gittin' my soul inter shape,
Gittin' my soul inter shape, fo' yo' see
Hit's a mighty big stone dat's layin' on me,
   Mighty big stone! Yes, indeedy!

I hope de good angel will hab heaps o' strength,
   Or else bring old Samson along,
Kase the sin on my soul's mo' 'en fo'ty foot deep;
Yo' see, I bin one ob dese wanderin' sheep,
   An' hit 's gwine ter need somebody strong,
Gwine ter need somebody strong, doan yo' see;
Hit's a mighty big weight dat's a restin' on me.
   Pow'ful big weight! Yes, indeedy!

I 'se gittin' my soul inter shape fo' de day
   When Peter 'gins takin' 'is toll;
Ready ter lay down my burden an' rest,
Ready ter take up de cross ob de blest,
   Ready ter entah de fol'.

Gittin' Inter Shape

Gittin' my soul inter shape, doan yo' see;
Dar's a big load ob sin bin restin' on me,
  Big load ob sin! Yes, indeedy!
    Yes, indeedy!

EVOLUTION

WE seem to exist in a hazardous time,
    Driftin' along here through space;
Nobody knows just when we begun
    Or how fur we've gone in the race.
Scientists argy we're shot from the sun,
    While others we're goin' right back,
An' some say we've allers been here more or less,
    An' seem to establish the fact.
O' course 'at's somepin' 'at nobody knows,
    As far as I've read or cun see;
An' them as does know all about the hull scheme,
    Why, none of 'em never agree.

Now, why I think it's a perilous time,—
    What do we know 'bout them spots
Up there on that glorious orb of the day?
    Smart men has argyed an' lots
Of the brainiest folks has been cypherin' out,
    An' all sorts of stories has riz

Evolution

'Bout what the sun 's made of or how it 's composed,
    An' lots of 'em think that it is.
O' course 'at 's somepin' 'at nobody knows—
    Nobody under the sun ;
Nary a body or bein', I s'pose ;
    Nary a bein' but One.

Take Eva Lution, an' what does she say
    'Bout how we all sprung from a ape ?
An' there's the goriller and big chimpanzee,
    Patterned exactly our shape.
An' I've seen some folks, an' I guess so have you,
    An' it ain't none of our bizness neither,
That actually looked like they sprung from a ape,
    An' did n't have fur to spring either.
Course 'at 's somepin 'at every one knows ;
    I do n't see how you folks can doubt it ;
S'posin' they have some resemblance to us,
    No use in a-writin' about it.

If a feller 'll take a geology book
    An' not go a rushin' long through it,
But jes' sort o' figger the thing out hisself—
    What I mean is : 'ply hisself to it—
He 'll see we 've dug up folks ten thousand years old,
    Built on a ponderous plan ;

Evolution

Somehow this knocks Mr. Moses all out,
   An' Adam, the biblical man.
O' course 'at 's somepin 'at nobody knows,
   Nobody under the sun ;
Nary a body or bein' I s'pose,
   Nary a bein' but One.

GEDDER IN YO' GRAIN

DE ole plow hoss is busy
    Breshin' flies off wid his tail,
De ole dog's got a move on him
Dat's zackly like a snail.
De meddeh grass is noddin'
En off yondah in de lane
I kin hyar de tree toads warnin'
"Bettah gedder in yo' grain."

Doan yo' hyar de frogs a-gurglin'
Dar out yondah in de pond?
What's de mattah wid de catbird,
Doan yo' hyar his voice respond?
Ain't de hull of 'em a-tellin' yo'
In language mighty plain,
"Doan be frivlin' way yo' moments,
Bettah gedder in yo' grain."

Ain't de bumble bee a-hummin'
'Mongst de clovah tops an' flowahs,

Gedder in Yo' Grain

Whilst de ole clock am a-tickin' 'way
De minutes an de houahs?
Chile, yo's got to be a-hus'lin'
To ketch de wisdom train.
Doan waste no opportunities,
But gedder in yo' grain.

JANE JONES

JANE JONES keeps talkin' to me all the time,
An' says you must make it a rule
To study your lessons 'nd work hard 'nd learn,
An' never be absent from school.
Remember the story of Elihu Burritt,
An' how he clum up to the top,
Got all the knowledge 'at he ever had
Down in a blacksmithing shop?
Jane Jones she honestly said it was so!
       Mebbe he did—
       I dunno!
O' course what's a-keepin' me 'way from the top,
Is not never havin' no blacksmithing shop.

She said 'at Ben Franklin was awfully poor,
But full of ambition an' brains;
An' studied philosophy all his hull life,
An' see what he got for his pains!
He brought electricity out of the sky,
With a kite an' a bottle an' key,

Jane Jones

An' we're owing him more'n any one else
For all the bright lights 'at we see.
Jane Jones she honestly said it was so !
      Mebbe he did—
         I dunno !
O' course what's allers been hinderin' me
Is not havin' any kite, lightning, er key.

Jane Jones said Abe Lincoln had no books at all
An' used to split rails when a boy ;
An' General Grant was a tanner by trade
An' lived way out in Ill'nois.
So when the great war in the South first broke out
He stood on the side o' the right,
An' when Lincoln called him to take charge o' things,
He won nearly every blamed fight.
Jane Jones she honestly said it was so !
      Mebbe he did—
         I dunno !
Still I ain't to blame, not by a big sight,
For I ain't never had any battles to fight.

She said 'at Columbus was out at the knees
When he first thought up his big scheme,
An' told all the Spaniards 'nd Italians, too,
An' all of 'em said 'twas a dream.

Jane Jones

But Queen Isabella jest listened to him,
'Nd pawned all her jewels o' worth,
'Nd bought him the Santa Maria 'nd said,
"Go hunt up the rest o' the earth!"
Jane Jones she honestly said it was so!
        Mebbe he did—
        I dunno!
O' course that may be, but then you must allow
They ain't no land to discover jest now!

ELOPEMENT

I'M out at the home of my Mary,
    Mary so young and so fair,
But her father and mother
And sister and brother
    And all of the family are there.

I'm now on the sofa with Mary,
    Mary with bright, golden hair;
But her father and mother
And sister and brother
    And all of the family are there.

I'm way up the river with Mary,
    Picnicking in the cool air;
But her father and mother
And sister and brother
    And all of the family are there.

I'm in the surf bathing with Mary;
    Her form is beyond compare;

Elopement

But her father and mother
And sister and brother
    And all of the family are there.

I'm down at the parson's with Mary;
    It's rather a private affair;
But her father and mother
And sister and brother
    Well—none of the family is there.

HER FOLKS AN' HIZ'N

HE maird her 'cause she had money an' some
    Property left from 'er husband's income;
But both of the families was awfully stirred,
An' said the worst things 'at the town ever heard.
        En her folks an' hiz'n,
        Er hiz'n an' her'n,
        Never spoke to each other,
        From what I can learn.

His folks begun it an' jest said 'at she
Was the worst actin' thing they ever did see;
An' ought to be ashamed fer bein' so bold,
'Cause her husband he had n't had time to get cold.
        En her folks an' hiz'n,
        Er hiz'n an' her'n,
        Never spoke to each other,
        From what I can learn.

Her folks they all set up 'at he was no good,
An' if 'twas n't for her—well, he 'd have to saw wood.

Her Folks An' Hiz'n

Then all of her kin, every blasted relation,
Said she'd lowered herself in their estimation.
    So her folks an' hiz'n,
    Er hiz'n an' her'n,
    Never spoke to each other,
    From what I can learn.

The sisters they told—this is 'tween you and I—
'At they thought she wanted her husband to die:
An' they whispered around—but do n't you lisp a
    word—
The awfulest things that a soul ever heard.
    So her folks an' hiz'n,
    Er hiz'n an' her'n,
    Never spoke to each other,
    From what I can learn.

They said that a travelin' man er a drummer,
Who stopped at the hotel a long time last summer,
That he—no it was n't that now—let me see—
That she—er something like that, seems to me.
    Well, her folks an' hiz'n,
    Er hiz'n an' her'n,
    Never spoke to each other,
    From what I can learn.

Her Folks An' Hiz'n

I hear 'at the families keep up the old fight,
A-roastin' each other from mornin' till night;
But the young maird couple they 've moved to the city,
Where gossip do n't go; but I think it a pity
      That her folks an' hiz'n,
      An' hiz'n an' her'n,
      Never speak to each other,
      From what I can learn.

THE YALLER JACKETS' NEST

IF I could only wander back
    To boyhood jest one day,
So'st' I could have my chice agin
    Of games we used to play,
I'd let the kites an' marbles go,
    An' say, "Come on, boys! let's
All go out a-huntin' fer
    The yaller jackets' nest."

Jest to lay up in the shadder
    Of the fence once agin
Of the old vacant lot
    'At the cows pastured in,
Where the dandelions were bloomin',
    'N there take a rest,
While you listen to the music
    'Round the yaller jackets' nest.

There was one 'at allers went along
    An' romped with us 'n raced,

The Yaller Jackets' Nest

With her sun-bonnet a-hangin' back
    'N curls down to 'er waist,
In the checkered little frock she wore
    Of gingham,—what a pest
She was to us when huntin' fer
    The yaller jackets' nest.

It's the prime of the blossoms
    'At's a-hangin' from the trees
An' the music of the buzzin'
    'At brings lonesome memories,
Fer it seems as if I heerd her say
    "You better look out, lest
They all swarm out and sting yeh
    From the yaller jackets' nest."

Sometimes I think I hear 'er voice
    An' see 'er eyes of blue,
That borried all their color from
    The sky 'at peeks at you
Between the clouds in summer
    After rain has fell an' blessed
The flowers an' openin' blossoms
    'Round the yaller jackets' nest.

HOW HANK DIED

"MOTHER, the shadows are gatherin' in,
   Shadows o' sunshine and shadows o' sin,
Shadows o' sorrow and shadows o' gloom,
All of 'em gatherin' now in my room.
See over there near the mantel-place wall
Is the darkest shadow.   What 's that—a call?
Oh, let in the light, keep that shadow away,
The one with the sickle that cuts to-day,
And far over there in the sunlands' West
I 'll work in the pastur' after I rest.

" Oh, to get out o' this valley o' sin
Up in the cool o' the hillside agin !
Where are the boys? All away? Where 's M'liss?
Who 's holdin' my hand, an' whose arm is this?
Oh, here comes the shadow that beckons—what pain !
It must not come near me!   Hear that?   That rain
On the windows? See, down by the foot-board, where
The curtain moves!   A shadow is there,
Comin' on tiptoe!   It 's after the light.
Oh, do n't give it welcome, that shadow of night !

How Hank Died

"Do n't leave me waitin' here now in the dark
The shadows are entering. What—music? Hark!
Can that be the soft winds of summer that send
Their sighs o'er the fields for the loss of a friend?
So cold? I am getting so cold, so cold.
Oh, why are the shadows so bold, so bold?
Here comes the grim shadow, the shadow of Death;
The cavern-eyed shadow that asks for my breath."
   * * * * *
"Good-bye," said the toiler; "good-bye every one."
Then somebody whispered: "The reaper is done."
His head fell back, and down by his side
His white hand dropped. That's how Hank died.

HOW OFTEN

THEY stood on the bridge at midnight,
    In a park not far from town;
They stood on the bridge at midnight
    Because they did n't sit down.

The moon rose o'er the city
    Behind the dark church spire;
The moon rose o'er the city
    And kept on rising higher.

How often, oh! how often
    They whispered words so soft;
How often, oh! how often,
    How often, oh! how oft.

BENTON HARBOR, MICH.

SOMETIMES I ain't a thing to do, an' so jist for the nonce,
I think of things I did n't see out on Midway Plaisance.
Although they claimed 'at every tribe an' nation, seems to me,
Was represented, yit there 's some I simply did n't see.
I went all through the Cairo Street, an' saw the Luxor great,
I saw the South Sea Islanders an' them from Congo State,
I saw the Patagonians, but, durn it all, my wish
Was more to see them funny folks from
                        Benton Harbor, Mich.

I took in all the bildin's that was prom'nent on the grounds,
Got in with a C'lumbian guard and we jist went the rounds.

Benton Harbor, Mich.

I says to him, "I 'm here this week to take the hull
    thing in;
I might not git a chance to go against the thing agin.
Outside o' horterculture an' some o' the smaller fruits
I want to see them Wolverines at 's still a-wearin'
    boots.
So don' show me no minin' er animals er fish,
I 'd rather see them curios from
                Benton Harbor, Mich."

What d' I care for foreign folks 'at come from pagan
    lands?
I 've heerd an' read enough of Paig, an' heerd the
    tom-tom bands.
I 've seen enough of Egypt, 'n Algiers, 'nd ancient
    Rome,
An' now I 'm jist a-spilin' for somepin' right 'round
    home.
Why, gosh all Friday! Take yer Turks an' all yer
    foreign kit,
I want to see them Wolverines, an' I ain't seen 'em
    yit;
Old Michigan I 'm after; seems as if I heerd the
    swish
Of breakers like I used to in
                Benton Harbor, Mich.

Benton Harbor, Mich.

So comin' out from there I says, "We'll take another route;
Course you may know your bizness, but I know what I'm about.
I'm on a hunt fer friends jist now, not Japs er Javanese,
Or sore-eyed Esquimaux, er Coons, er bias-eyed Chinese.
I've heerd enough of 'Hot! hot! hot!' got frightened at the roar
'Round Hagenbeck's, an' shook hands with the Sultan of Johore,
Until I'm simply tired out, an' now my only wish
Is jist to see them old-time folks from
                    Benton Harbor, Mich."

I walked till I got dusty an' thought I'd like to wash,
When lookin' up I saw a tower—'t was Michigan, by gosh!
"Come on," I says, "I'll show you now some folks you never saw,
Human bein's from Muskegon, Dowagiac, an' Saginaw;

Benton Harbor, Mich.

Them folks 'at raises celery 'way out in Kal'mazoo,
Cassopolis, an' Globeville, an' Ypsilanti, too—
St. Joe an' Berrien Centre." I guess I got my
    wish,
I jined the jays an' we went back to
                      Benton Harbor, Mich.

ASPHODEL

Carest thou naught for me, lone Asphodel?
Oh, flower! Shall all the summer days long gone
Roll into space remembered not? What spell,
Nay, more, what dream, what fantasy is this?
E'en one small hour to gaze and love. 'Tis bliss
Like Gyges knew behind the chamber door
In days of old. Those mellow days of yore.

Ah, no, sweet flower, say not farewell, I pray;
But let thine odor loiter yet a while,
And linger thou beside my lonely way,
Spreading thy perfume. And each tender leaf,
Sparkling with dew, like tears in eyes of grief;
Eager am I to pluck thee from thy stem,
To have thee near, and in thy fragrance dwell,
Trusting thee ever, fairy Asphodel.

THE FLOWERS' BALL

THERE is an olden story,
   'Tis a legend, so I'm told,
How the flowerets gave a banquet,
   In the ivied days of old;
How the posies gave a party once
   That wound up with a ball,
How they held it in a valley,
   Down in "Flowery Kingdom Hall."

The flowers of every clime were there,
   Of high and low degree,
All with their petals polished,
   In sweet aromatic glee.
They met down in this woodland
   In the soft and ambient air,
Each in its lolling loveliness,
   Exhaled a perfume rare.

An orchestra of Blue Bells
   Sat upon a mossy knoll

The Flowers' Ball

And pealed forth gentle music
    That quite captured every soul.
The Holly hocked a pistil
    Just to buy a suit of clothes,
And danced with all the flowerets
    But the modest, blushing Rose.

The Morning Glory shining
    Seemed reflecting all the glow
Of dawn, and took a partner ;
    It was young Miss Mistletoe.
Miss Maggie Nolia from the South
    Danced with Forget-me-not ;
Sweet William took Miss Pink in tow
    And danced a slow gavotte.

Thus everything went swimmingly
    'Mongst perfumed belles and beaux,
And every floweret reveled save
    The modest, blushing Rose.
Miss Fuchsia sat around and told
    For floral emulation,
That she had actually refused
    To dance with A. Carnation.

The Flowers' Ball

The Coxcomb, quite a dandy there,
    Began to pine and mope,
Until he had been introduced
    To young Miss Heliotrope.
Sir Cactus took Miss Lily,
    And he swung her so about
She asked Sweet Pea to Cauliflower
    And put the Cactus out.

Miss Pansy took her Poppy
    And she waltzed him down the line
Till they ran against old Sunflower
    With Miss Honeysuckle Vine.
The others at the party that
    Went whirling through the mazy
Were the Misses Rhodo Dendron,
    Daffodil and little Daisy.

Miss Petunia, Miss Verbena, Violet,
    And sweet Miss Dahlia
Came fashionably late, arrayed
    In very rich regalia.
Miss Begonia, sweet Miss Buttercup,
    Miss Lilac and Miss Clover;
Young Dandelion came in late
    When all the feast was over.

The Flowers' Ball

The only flower that sent regrets
   And really could n't come,
Who lived in the four hundred, was
   The vain Chrysanthemum.
One floweret at the table
   Grew quite ill, we must regret,
And every posy wondered, too,
   Just what Miss Mignonette.

Young Tulip chose Miss Orchid
   From the first, and did not part
With her until Miss Mary Gold
   Fell with a Bleeding Heart.
But ah ! Miss Rose sat pensively
   Till every young bud passed her ;
When just to fill the last quadrille,
   The little China Aster.

DE SUN'S COMIN' BACK

Hush! chillun, hush!
    Kase de sun's done come back agin,
Back agin a-shinin' on de ole cypress tree;
        Hush! chillun, hush!
    Hit shuahly am a fac' agin,
    De sun's done come back agin,
Back agin to me.

        Hush! chillun, hush!
    Foh de sun's done come back agin,
Pushin' yaller glory roun' in ebbery spot it finds,
    Dancin' on de cradle
    An' old Chloe wid de ladle,
    An' coaxin' out de blossoms on
De honeysuckle vines.

        Hush! chillun, hush!
    Kase de sof' winds come back agin,
Back agin, a-bringin' all de glory ob de spring;

De Sun's Comin' Back

    My heart's jes' a-throbbin'
    For off yondah is de robin,
      An' de blackbird am a-cluckin'
An' I 'low I heerd 'im sing.

        Hush! chillun, hush!
    Kase de sun's done come back agin,
Bringin' back de fac' agin I 'se gittin' mighty old;
      I often sit and pondah,
      An' I wondah, an' I wondah,
    How many times it 's comin' back
Befo' I reach de fold.

THE RIVER ST. JOE

WHERE the bumblebee sips and the clover is red,
And the zephyrs come laden with peachblow perfume,
Where the thistle-down pauses in search of the rose
And the myrtle and woodbine and wild ivy grows;
Where the catbird pipes up and it sounds most divine
Off there in the branches of some lonely pine;
Oh, give me the spot that I once used to know
By the side of the placid old River St. Joe!

How oft on its banks I have sunk in a dream,
Where the willows bent over me kissing the stream,
My boat with its nose sort of resting on shore,
While the cat-tails stood guarding a runaway oar;
It appeared like to me, that they sort of had some
Way of knowing that I would soon get overcome,
With the meadow lark singing just over the spot
I did n't care whether I floated or not—
Just resting out there for an hour or so
On the banks of the tranquil old River St. Joe.

The River St. Joe

Where the tall grasses nod at the close of the day,
And the sycamore's shadow is slanting away—
Where the whip-poor-will chants from a far distant
    limb
Just as if the whole business was all made for him.
Oh! it's now that my thoughts, flying back on the
    wings
Of the rail and the die-away song that he sings,
Brings the tears to my eyes that drip off into rhyme,
And I live once again in the old summer time;
For my soul it seems caught in old time's under-tow
And I'm floating away down the River St. Joe.

BABY UP AT BATTENBERG'S

HEERD 'bout what 's happened?
    Why o' course ye has;
Baby up at Battenberg's,
Hope it tain 't the las'!

Doctor come at eight o'clock,
Rig all spleshed with clay;
Dad a trampin' up the hall,
Skeery?—I sh'd say!

Kind o' still 'roun' the house,
Folks on tiptoe walk
Tell the door is open
An' we hear a squawk!

Doctor whispers suthin'—
Daddy hollers: "No!"
Doctor says, "Twelve pounder!"
Daddy whoops out: "Sho!"

Daddy—happier 'n a clam!
Mother doin' well;
Baby up at Battenberg's,
Have n't ye heerd tell?

Upon the death of the late Lord Tennyson, Mr. King fancied himself an applicant for the position of Poet Laureate and produced this poem as his recommendation to the Appointing Power.

NO HARM DONE

EXCUSE me, Mr. Handy, for a-droppin' you a line,
But the fact is, I've arrived in town and feelin' mighty fine;
I'm stoppin' at the Press Club, er that's where I take my meals,
An' I must say I'm agitatin' some colossal deals;
But what I want to ask you is, 'at seems a-botherin' me,
Is your hippodrome at Jackson Park, that's what I want to see;
I'd lay all careful pains aside an' wear a steady grin
'F I thought 'at you could work some scheme
      Of gittin' of me in.
    Course, if you say they isn't,
      I'll say I's just in fun,
    An' we'll just let it go at that—
      They's no harm done.

No Harm Done

Say, Handy, what I want is so 's I can push my phiz
All 'round the hull World's Fair grounds an see
  everything they is,
An' when a C'lumbian guard comes up unmannerly
  and gruff,
I 'll flash the pass you give me, Handy, that 'll be
  enough,
An' passin' on an' mirrorin' my face in the lagoon
Where that fellow is a-standin'—now what 's his
  name ?—Neptune.
I want to see you, Major, yes, I want to grasp your
  fin,
'Cause I know 'at you could work some scheme
      Of gittin' of me in.
     Course, if you say they is n't,
      I 'll say I 's just in fun,
     An' we 'll just let it go at that—
      They 's no harm done.

I want to see the state buildin's an' all ther' is there,
I want to see that queer machine that turns out com-
  pressed air,
Th' Administration Buildin' an' th' Agricultural Hall—
I tell you, Major, hones'ly, I want to see it all.
I 'll be alone mos' of the time an' nothin' 's goin' to
  please

No Harm Done

Me better than to get acquainted with those Javanese.
Do n't say a word! Say, Handy, I must brace you agin:
Is they any possibility
        Of gittin' of me in?
      Course, if you say they is n't,
        I 'll say I 's just in fun,
     An' we 'll just let it go at that—
      They 's no harm done.

I 've read the weekly papers, Major, out at old St. Joe,
They ain't been nothin' in 'em 'at the country folks do n't know.
Some wants to see machinery, some paintin's, an' some fish,
Some want to hear the music, too, but I tell you my wish
Is just to see them foreign girls from Spain an' sunny France,
An' Abdul Something, what-'s-his-name, that 's got them girls 'at dance
Out there in Midway Plaisance, an' the Sultan an' his kin.
Oh, Handy, you must fix some scheme
        Of gittin' of me in.

No Harm Done

Course, if you say they is n't,
 I 'll say I 's just in fun,
An' we 'll just let it go at that—
 They 's no harm done.

THE FATES

FORTUNE came to a youth one day and dressed 'im
Up in his best. While Society smiled and caressed 'im,
Along came Toil with a hammer and saw to test 'im—
        And all three pressed 'im.

Manhood came, as it usually does, to beard 'im;
Virtue stole in and sat by his side, but feared 'im;
Ambition came with wonderful schemes and steered 'im—
        But all three queered 'im.

Wisdom came and knocked at his door; he spurned 'im.
Frivolity came on bicycle wheels and turned 'im;
Remorse at last came up and stung 'im and burned 'im—
        And all three churned 'im.

The Fates

Poverty opened his door and found 'im and sought 'im ;
Paralysis, crouched in a corner, had finally caught 'im ;
Idleness claimed the prize because she 'd taught 'im—
        But all three got 'im.

Old Charon rowed up in Time's canoe and ferried 'im
Over the creek, when an undertaker hurried 'im,
Dropped sand on his box, while a parson talked and worried 'im—
        But the whole crowd buried 'im.

PARAPHRASE

THE master of the manor house each morn
   Upon his shining steed through arbored gates
Rides forth and out upon the dusty road
To yon small hamlet smiling on the hill.
At eve rides back with swaying form ; he meets
The faithful footman, and, his charger placed,
He wends his way into the mansion hall,
While I, down here in meadow lands all day,
   I only s-s-stack the hay.

The opulent lord when mellow days are come,
At the high note of the red-combed chanticleer,
With horse and hound and merry crowd now bent
Upon the chase. Swift through fox-scented roads,
Stopping, perchance, at many a wayside inn,
The music of the jingling glass is his,
While I down here in perfumed clover fields,
Hear but the music of the lark and jay.
   I only s-s-stack the hay.

Paraphrase

Lone is the mansion on the sunlit hill,
Save for the daughter of the chivalric lord,
Who comes now, finger-kissed by high-topped
  sheaves
(Pausing the while, half startled by the quail)
To where the haycocks dot the sallow fields ;
Comes in the roseate flush of maidenhood ;
Comes with a truant smile upon her lips,
And romping up to me exclaiming : "Say !"
    B-b-but I—I only s-s-stack the hay.

Then spake she soft as runs a summer brook
Or novel of some scribe of amorous mind :
" How far the huntsmen must be on the road,
Because the sun comes through my window-blind ;
Within—strange creakings 'bout the halls : with-
  out—
The scurrying leaves. So lonely am I now
I've wandered here to ask whate'er betide.
Wouldst cease thy work ? Pray, must you toil
  to-day ?"
" W-w-well, yes," I s-s-say, " I have t-t-to s-s-stack
  the hay."

" Ah, sir !" she then replied : " A banquet spread
But yesternight for me with many guests

Paraphrase

And suitors gathered 'round the festal board
Sought ardently my hand; and one forth brought
A golden cup in memory of my birth.
Yea, each in quest of all these lands. Kind sir,
How now; wouldst thou not drink from out my
 cup?
Prithee, come solace me! Live while you live,
 for aye."
" I c-c-ca-ca-can't," I s-s-say. "I have to s-s-stack
 the hay."

The days roll on and now a blasé youth
Rides by the manor house. A reaper he
In wisdom's fields. No importuning maid
Bade him alight. She beckons. Quick he opes
The gates, and, hastening to the banquet halls,
He drinks to her, and, pledging endless love,
They fly to distant parish. Now the hills
And vales and lands that roll away are his.
While I, down here in meadow-lands all day,
 I only s-s-stack the hay.

IF I CAN BE BY HER

I D-D-DO N'T c-c-c-are how the r-r-r-obin sings,
Er how the r-r-r-ooster f-f-flaps his wings,
Er whether 't sh-sh-shines, er whether 't pours,
Er how high up the eagle s-s-soars,
    If I can b-b-b-be by her.

I do n't care if the p-p-p-people s-say,
'At I 'm weak-minded every-w-way,
An' n-n-never had no cuh-common sense,
I 'd c-c-c-cuh-climb the highest p-picket fence
    If I could b-b-b-be by her.

If I can be by h-h-her, I 'll s-s-swim
The r-r-r-est of life thro' th-th-thick an' thin ;
I 'll throw my overcoat away,
An' s-s-s-stand out on the c-c-c-oldest day,
    If I can b-b-b-be by her.

You s-s-see sh-sh-she weighs an awful pile,
B-b-b-but I d-d-d-do n't care—sh-she 's just my style,

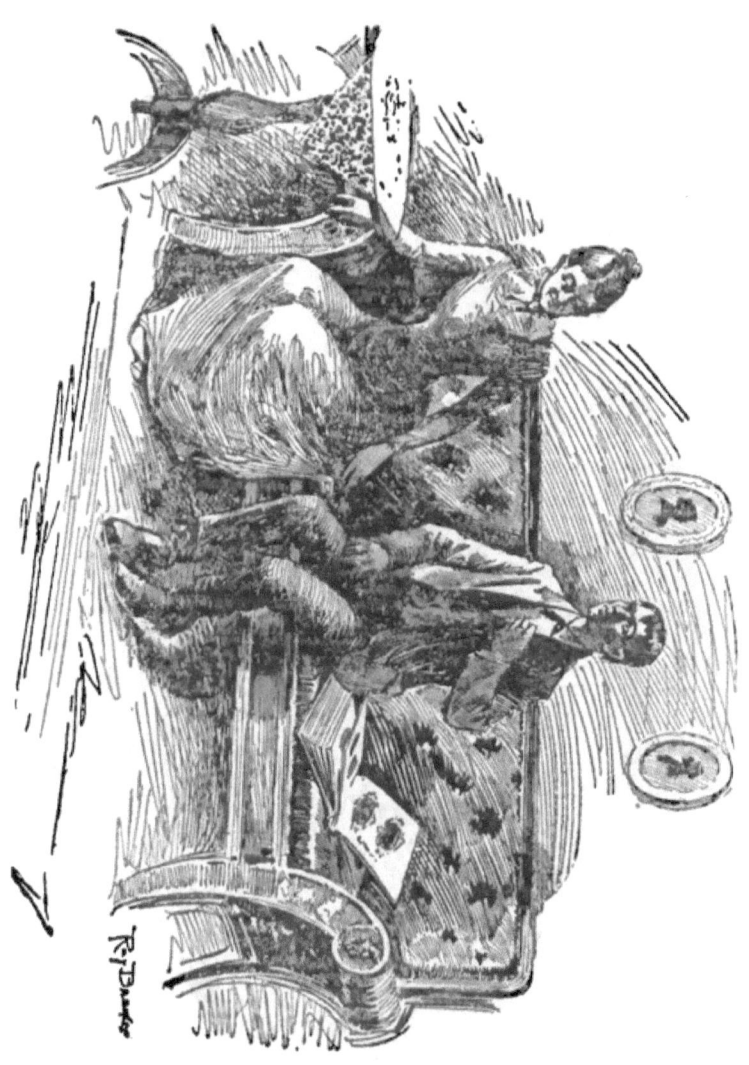

If I Can Be By Her

An' any f-f-fool could p-p-p-lainly see
She'd look well b-b-b-by the side of me,
    If I could b-b-b-be by her.

I b-b-b-braced right up, and had the s-s-s-and
To ask 'er f-f-f-father f-f-fer 'er hand ;
He said : "Wh-wh-what p-p-prospects have you
    got ?"
I said : "I gu-gu-guess I've got a lot,
    If I can b-b-b-be by her."

It's all arranged f-f-fer Christmas Day,
Fer then we're goin' to r-r-r-run away,
An' then s-s-some th-th-thing that cu-cu-couldn't be
At all b-b-efore will then, you s-s-see,
    B-b-b-because I'll b-b-b-be by her.

TOBOGGAN

DOWN from the hills and over the snow
    Swift as a meteor's flash we go,
  Toboggan! Toboggan! Toboggan!
Down from the hills with our senses lost,
Jealous of cheeks that are kissed by the frost,
  Toboggan! Toboggan! Toboggan!

With snow piled high on housetop and hill,
O'er frozen rivulet, river, and rill,
Clad in her jacket of sealskin and fur,
Down from the hills I'm sliding with her,
  Toboggan! Toboggan! Toboggan!

Down from the hills, what an awful speed!
As if on the back of a frightened steed,
  Toboggan! Toboggan! Toboggan!
Down from the hills at the rise of the moon,
Merrily singing the toboggan tune,
  "Toboggan! Toboggan! Toboggan!"

Toboggan

Down from the hills like an arrow we fly,
Or a comet that whizzes along through the sky;
Down from the hills! Oh, is n't it grand!
Clasping your best winter girl by the hand,
    Toboggan! Toboggan! Toboggan!

Down from the hills and both growing old,
Down from the hills we are nearing the fold:
    Toboggan! Toboggan! Toboggan!
Close to the homestead we hear the ring
Of children's voices that cheerily sing,
    "Toboggan! Toboggan! Toboggan!"

Down from the hills and we hear the chime
Of bells that are ringing out Old Father Time;
Down from the hills we are riding away,
Nearing the life with its endless day;
    Toboggan! Toboggan! Toboggan!

DE BUGLE ON DE HILL

I DOAN like de noise ob de marchin' ob de boys,
    An' I 'low doan s'pose I evah will;
Er de trampin' ob de feet to de drum's wild beat,
    Er de sound ob de bugle on de hill.
Hit 'minds me ob de day when Gabe marched away
    En ole missus stood beside de cabin do';
Somepin' whispahed in my ear 'bout my little volunteer,
    An' said he nevah will come back no mo'.

I 'membah now de day jes' how he marched away,
    Wid de bright sun er climbin' up de sky,
Marched out en down de street to de drum's wild beat,
    Den dey fotched him home to die.
Oh, de sad en moanful way, po' old missus kneeled ter pray,
    When Gabe said: "Hit's gittin' mighty still."

It is an interesting fact to note that this is the first poem by a Chicago author to be printed in "The Century Magazine."

De Bugle On De Hill

But I rise en jine de boys when I hear de cannon's
    noise,
    Er de blowin' ob de bugle on de hill.

Hit 'pears es if I seen de ole plantation green,
    En sometimes I sho'ly think I hear
De regiment pars by, en 'low I hear de cry
    En de moan ob my little volunteer.
En I see de moanful way po' ole missus kneel to pray,
    En sometimes when all aroun' is still,
I kin hear de tread ob feet to de drum's wild beat
    En de blowin' ob de bugle on de hill.

Dar's a spot mighty dear to dis ole darky here,
    Whar de sunlight is peepin' froo de palms,
Wid his hands 'pon his breast, dar my soldier's gone
    to rest,
    Jes' peacefully er sleepin' in de calms.
En de drum's wild beat er de tread ob marchin' feet
    No mo' kain't disturb 'im now until
De Lord gibs command, den I know he'll rise en
    stand
    At de sound ob de bugle on de hill.

OLD ST. JOE

OF all the towns that jest suits me
From Stevensville to Manistee,
There's one old place I can't fergit;
It ain't a great ways off, and yit
From here it's sixty miles or so
In a bee line—that's Old St. Joe.

I don't p'tend to write, an' ain't
One of them air chaps 't paint;
'F I was I'd tell of scenes 't lie
Stretched out afore a feller's eye;
Er when the sun was hangin' low
I'd paint it right from Old St. Joe.

I've seen folks gether thare in crowds
Jist fer to watch the golden clouds
Changin' shapes, and sort o' windin'
Into figgers, never mindin'
That old lake spread out below,
Reflectin' 'em at Old St. Joe.

Old St. Joe

Underneath them cedar trees
'S where I used to take my ease.
Birds a-singin' all along
The hedge, an' each one had a song
An' sung its best to let you know
They jist got back to Old St. Joe.

They ain't no purtier site to me—
That is, 'cordin' to my idee—
Than jist to watch the gulls 'at fly
Round that old pier; an' hear 'em cry
An' circle round. It 'pears they know
Fishin's good at Old St. Joe.

Course the people over there
They don't notice 'em or care—
What they're worryin' 'bout is frost,
'N whether strawberries is lost;
Yet they 'pear to take things slow,
Jist the same as Old St. Joe.

'Ceptin' rheumatiz, their health
Is middlin' good, an' as fer wealth
They got that, an' lots o' land;
'Course the sile is mixed 'ith sand;
But that's what makes the berries grow
Over there at Old St. Joe.

Old St. Joe

Take it gener'ly, as a rule,
A feller likes where it's cool,
Where he can sleep, an' drink in air
That comes perfumed from orchards where
The peach trees jist begin to blow ;
Then where's a place like Old St. Joe ?

Such cool breeze blowin' back
Keeps the skeeters makin' tack
'N the flies they mostly stay
Up round Pipestone creek, they say.
Tell you what, one thing I know—
They ain't no flies on Old St. Joe.

THE TRAMP

HE came from where he started
    And was going where he went.
He had n't had a smell of food,
    Not even had a scent.
He never even muttered once
    Till he began to talk,
And when he left the kitchen door
    He took the garden walk.

He said: "There's no one with me,
    Because I am alone;
I might have scintillated once;
    My clothes have always shone.
I got here 'fore the other ones
    Because I started first:
The reason I look shabby is
    Because I 'm dressed the worst."

Then I asked him where he came from—
    This was just before we parted,
And he muttered indistinctly,
    "Oh, I come from where I started!"

THE CHAUTAUQUAN MAID

SHE had studied every ology—
Ichthyology, zoölogy,
Philology, geology, conchology, and more;
Knew the bones of every mammal,
From the mouse up to the camel,
And the mollusks and crustaceans that crept on every shore.

To think her up in history
Was not at all a mystery;
She could name you any ruler from old England to Sumatra.
It would certainly amaze you
What she said about Aspasia
And the little unsophisticated maiden, Cleopatra.

She had studied Greek and Latin,
Hebrew, Sanscrit (please put that in);
Read Xenophon and Horace, Ovid, Virgil and the rest.

The Chautauquan Maid

She did n't say, "I 'll learn yuh,"
But "teach you" that Calphurnia
Sewed fifty-seven buttonholes in Julius Cæsar's vest.

She loved to pull the petals
From a flower. The baser metals,
She doted on their study, and for nuggets she would
    bone you.
She loved the dromedary,
And the docile cassowary,
And the feathers of the emu she had stuck in her
    "chiffonier."

She had studied evolution,
And arrived at the solution
How long our first appendage was; of course, I
    did n't ask her,
But she said that she 'd resolved from
What she knew, that I evolved from
A carrot-haired chimpanzee she had seen in Madagascar.

She could scan iambic meter,
And she knew each Roman prætor,
And surprised me when she told the way the empire
    came to fall.

The Chautauquan Maid

The Huns sneaked in the forum,
And the Romans tried to floor 'em,
But they got themselves in trouble, and, of course,
   got whipped, by Gaul.

I'M A BLUEJAY

I'M a bluejay, 'nd never mind
'F my toe does stick out behind.
   When I ketch on a limb
   I'm there for keeps—
   'Lesn I let go.
Of course I must eat.
   Sometimes, you know,
   I have to jes' let go
   O' that hind toe.

I'm a dead sure thing in spring.
As soon 's the weather 's kind o' warm
   You'll notice me on a fence.
   I feel immense
   In my blue suit.
The woods can ketch my chirp;
   You hear my toot
From then out 'f you do n't shoot
   At my blue suit.

I'm a Bluejay

I put ripe cherries in my face,
Same place I wedge all the bugs;
   An' do n't you ever think
   'At I 'm no good
   An' sponge my way.
Do I? I guess I 'll fool yuh,
   I eat yer durn "circulia."
   I guess I work my way
   'F I am a jay.

'RASTUS KING

AS you happen jes' to mention
    Old time friends 'at sort o' bring
Mem'ries back, I'd like to ask
    What's become o' 'Rastus King?

Did he go out west prospectin'
    Far on Californy's rim?
Did he settle with the Injuns,
    Or did the Injuns settle him?

What a great big-hearted feller
    'Rastus was, and how he'd sing!
Sometimes tears 'll start to rollin'
    When I think o' 'Rastus King.

Where is he an' what's come of him?
    Is he toilin' hard fer bread?
Is he prosperous and wealthy?
    Is he livin' still, or dead?

How my heart recalls the mornin'
    That I met him. Splittin' wood,

'Rastus King

Payin' fer his school tuition,
  Earnin' thus a livelihood.

Allers boarded at the neighbors,
  Turned his hand at anything ;
Faithful, honest ; well the farmers
  Simply swore by 'Rastus King.

Find him down to meetin' Sundays
  Sittin' in the deacon's pew ;
Talk about yer knowledge ; he had
  Read the Bible through and through.

When the choir would jine together
  An' with the congregation sing,
Way above all other voices
  You could hear 'im—'Rastus King.

Did you ever come to meet 'im ?
  Do you think he 's livin' here ?
Say, he ain't much older 'n I am ;
  Reckon now he 's sixty year.

Last I heerd he 's doin' splendid,
  Rich, fast horses, everything.
Jest like him, a regular schemer ;
  Oh ! I knew him, 'Rastus King.

'Rastus King

Then the hackman I'd been asking
   All these questions thus did say :
" Rastus livin' purty quiet ;
   Don't go out at all, they say."

" Don't go out at all—why, stranger ?
   What's the matter?   Did he fail ?"
" Well," said he, " nothin's the matter,
   Stephen, only he's in jail."

THAT VALENTINE

ONCE, I remember, years ago,
    I sent a tender valentine;
I know it caused a deal of woe.
Once, I remember, years ago,
Her father's boots were large, you know.
    I do regret the hasty line,
Once, I remember, years ago
    I sent a tender valentine.

I know I never can forget
    I sent the tender valentine;
Somehow or other I regret,
But how I never can forget,
But then, I know, I know I met
    Her father. Oh, what grief was mine.
I know I never shall forget
    I sent a tender valentine.

DE GOOD SHIP

I'SE bin watchin' long fer de Good Ship,
   De Good Ship de Lo'd sent ter me ;
An' it 'pears dat hit's had a long voyage
   Crossin' life's troublesome sea.

I'se spected it 'long in de moh'nin',
   When nary a sail was in sight,
An' I'se looked fer it 'long about noonday,
   'N watched fer it way in de night.

Till I cast my eye ovah de boun'less
   Ole ocean, an' what did I see ?
Off der in de hush ob de distance
   De Good Ship a-comin' to me.

So I laid my haid down on my pillow,
   Fo'gettin' life's worry an' sin ;
An' when I awoke in de moh'nin',
   My Good Ship had done got in.

A CASUAL OBSERVATION

DAR'S nuffin' hyar but vanity
    An' riches an' insanity;
De dollah seems to be de people's god.
    Dar's a heap too many 'Scariots
    A-ridin' 'roun' in chariots,
While de po' man am a-carryin' de hod.

    Dar's too much haste an' hurryin',
    An' too much wealth at buryin',
An' dis hyar t'ing am gettin' worse and worse,
    Hit takes all ob de rakin's,
    De scrimpin's an' de scrapin's
To liquidate de 'spenses ob de hearse.

    Dar's heaps ob care an' worry;
    Ebberybody's in a hurry,
An' de few am growin' richer ebbery day;
    But de most of us must shovel
    For de children in de hovel
An' silently await de judgment day.

LIKE THE NEW FRIENDS BEST

DON'T talk to me o' old time friends,
    But jes give me the new.
The old friends may be good enough,
But somehow they won't do,
I do n't care for their old time ways;
Their questions you 'll allow
Are soulless as a parrot's gab:—
"Well, what you up to now?"
That's one thing I 've agin 'em,
'Cause that with all the rest,
Like hintin' 'bout some old time debt;
I like my new friends best.

I meet an old friend in the street,
As oftentimes I do,
Mechanically he stops to shake
An' say: "Well, how are you?"
Then drawin' down his face, as if
His cheeks was filled with lead,
He says: "I spose you 've heard the news?"

Like the New Friends Best

"No!"   "Eli Stubbs is dead.
An' 'fore he died he ast for you—
Seemed sorry you was gone,
An' said 'at what he 'd let you have
He hoped would help you on."
Now that's why I do n't like 'em much,
You prob'bly might have guessed.
I aint got much agin' 'em, but
I like the new friends best.

Old friends are most too home-like now.
They know your age, and when
You got expelled from school, and lots
Of other things, an' then
They 'member when you shivereed
The town an' broke the lights
Out of the school 'nen run away
An' played "Hunt Cole" out nights.
They 'member when you played around
Your dear old mommy's knee;
It's them can tell the very date
That you got on a spree.
I do n't like to forget 'em, yet
If put right to the test
Of hankerin' right now for 'em,
I like the new friends best.

A NEGRO SONG OF HOME

'TAIN'T berry many people wat 'll listen to a niggah
   Un 'low dey's enny sense in wot he say,
But I'se gwine ter guv de 'sperience of mah feelin's, and I figgah
   Dat dey's quite a smart o' people tinks mah way.
W'en a man begins a-shoutin' 'bout de good tings dat he 's missin'
   Kickin' kase dey ain't a fortune in his job,
Let 'im go home to his kitchen, an' set down a while an' listen
   To de singin' ob de kettle on de hob.

I 've hayrd de strains ob "Home, Sweet Home" when Patti was a-singin'
   An' de aujience was a-spillin' ob deir tears;
But I did n't mind the singah, fo' a different tune kep' ringin'
   Wif hits ha'nty kin' ob music in mah ears.

A Negro Song of Home

An' I reckernized de melerdy so powerful bewitchin'
  Dat made mah heart like sixty fo' ter t'rob,
An' I mejiate felt a hank'rin' fo' my cozy little kitchen
  An' de singin' ob de kettle on de hob.

De rich man can inhabitate a palace ef he wishes,
  Wif brick-er-brack and pictuahs on de wall ;
An' kin lay on velvet sofers an' eat off'n golden dishes,
  But I would n't swap mah kitchen fo' his all ;
Fo' hit would n't be like home ter me but 'ceptin' I could listen,
  A-puffin' at de backy in mah cob,
While de good Lawd seemed a-speakin' ob a home-like kin' ob blessin'
  Frough de singin' ob de kettle on de hob.

S'POSIN'

WHAT if the new San Francisco should sail
    To Chilian waters away,
With the Boston and Yorktown afar in the east,
    'Nd the Lancaster off in Bombay;
'Nd the big Philadelphia—s'posin' she wuz
    A-loadin' with tea in Japan,
With the Concord and Bennington flyin' so gay
    Their colors around Hindostan;
'Nd s'posin' the Charleston wuz in Bering Sea,
    With the Newark in Pamlico Sound,
'Nd the Miantonomah's big bilers should bust,
    'Nd the Baltimore run hard aground;
Then s'posin' we got in a fight right away
    With Chili or even Peru,
'Nd England should work the shell game on New York,
    Say—what in the deuce would we do?

LITTLE 'RASMUS

DE Great Good Speret come down from above
An' took leetle 'Rasmus away;
Took my leetle 'Rasmus dat played peep wid me,
En rode out to Banbury Cross on my knee,
    Took po' leetle 'Rasmus away.
Took my leetle 'Rasmus dat played roun' de do'
An' danced at de sunbeams dat fell on de flo',
    Took my leetle 'Rasmus away.

Dat 's why I 'se down-hearted an' kain't fin' relief,
An' ol' an' bent over; I 'se loaded with grief
    Kase 'Rasmus has done gone away.
De Great Good Speret comes down from de sky
An' hovahs aroun' ebbery day,
An' hit 'pears what yo 's lovin' a leetle too much,
De Good Speret takes it away,
    Kase He took leetle 'Rasmus away.

But I know de Good Speret mus' be mighty glad,
But dis darky's heart am jes' mounful an' sad
    Since 'Rasmus has done gone away.

Little 'Rasmus

An' mos'ly at morn, when de whimperin' breeze
Am loiterin' up in de sycamore trees,
An' at noon when de sun dances roun' on de flo'
Dis ole darky's heart am jes' burdened wid woe,
An' at night twixt de win' an' de patterin' rain,
My po' soul an' body am restless wid pain
    Since 'Rasmus has done gone away.

But I know de Good Speret comes down from de sky
An' hovahs aroun' ebbery day,
An' hit 'pears what yo' worship a leetle too much
De Good Speret takes it away,
Kase He took leetle 'Rasmus away—
    Took po' leetle 'Rasmus away.

NOBODY KNOWS

NOBODY knows when de col' winds am blowin',
Whar all de po' little chillun am a-goin'.
Nobody knows when de night time's hoverin'
How many little ones am des'tute ob coverin'.
Nobody sees, but de Lo'd done see 'em,
An' bime-by de Lo'd 'll tell humanity ter free 'em.

Nobody knows jes' how many am in rags,
A-sleepin' in de hot blocks an' 'roun' on de flags,
Nobody sees all dis poverty an' woe,
A-livin' on de emptyin's an' not a place ter go.
Nobody sees, but de Lo'd done see 'em,
An' bime-by de Lo'd 'll tell humanity ter free 'em.

Nobody knows whar dis poverty all comes—
How many po' folk am sleepin' in de slums.
Nobody knows jes' how few am befriendin',
But de good Lo'd knows dar mus' soon be an endin'.
Nobody sees, but de Lo'd done see 'em,
An' bime-by de Lo'd 'll tell humanity ter free 'em.

SHE DOES NOT HEAR

SH-SH-SH-SH-SHE does not hear the r-r-r-r-robin
    sing,
Nor f-f-f-f-feel the b-b-b-b-balmy b-b-breath of
    Spring;
Sh-sh-sh-she does not hear the p-p-pelting rain
B-b-b-beat ta-ta-tat-t-t-toos on the w-w-winder
    p-p-pane.

Sh-sh-sh-she cuc-cuc-cannot see the Autumn s-s-sky,
Nor hear the wild geese s-s-s-stringing b-b-by;
And, oh! how happy t-t-t- 'tis to know
Sh-sh-she never f-f-feels an earthly woe!

I s-s-spoke to her; sh-sh-she would not speak.
I kuk-kuk-kuk-kissed her, but c-c-cold was her cheek.
I could not twine her w-w-w-wondrous hair—
It w-w-was so wonderf-f-f-fully rare.

B-b-beside her s-s-stands a v-v-v-vase of flowers,
A gilded cuc-cuc-cuc-clock that t-t-tells the hours;

She Does Not Hear

And even now the f-f-fire-light f-f-f-falls
On her, and d-d-dances on the walls.

Sh-sh-she's living in a p-p-pup-purer life,
Where there's no tu-tuh-turmoil and no strife;
No t-t-t-tongue can m-m-m-mock, no words em-
    barrass
Her b-b-b-b-by g-g-gosh! she's p-p-plaster paris!

DOWN THE MISSISSIPPI

OH, de ole plantation landin',
    On de Mississippi sho',
'Pears es if I seed ole massa
    Standin' waitin' dar once mo'—
Back aways to whar de cabin's
    Almos' hid by lilac trees—
Seems es ef I h'yard po' missus
    Singin' old-time melodies.

Hollyhocks en honeysuckles
    Grow en bloom along de way,
Leadin' up dar to de cabin;
    But de ole folks, whar are dey?
An' de winin' path a-leadin'
    Roun' de house; sometimes, a spell,
Seems es ef I h'yard de win'less
    H'istin' watah f'om de well.

Down the Mississippi

Cap'n, kain yo' stop de boat, sah?
    Stop de boat, kase well I know
I has done gone down dis rivah
    'Bout es far 's hi keah ter go.
You kin lan' me soon 's yo 's ready,
    En I 'low I 'll fin' mah way
Back to dat ole shattah'd homestead
    Whar de sun shines froo to-day.

Massa Lincoln's gunboats let' it
    Jais dat way in sixty-three;
Cose dey did some monsus damage,
    But dey set us dahkies free.
How I 'membah po' ole missus
    Standin' n'yah de cabin do'
En she say: "Yo' gwine off, 'Rasmus?
    Ain' yo' gwine come back no mo'?"

Den I sade: "Not zackly, missus;
    Somepin 's done ketched ontah me.
Dar 's a big stampede ob darkies
    From Kaintuck en Tennessee.
When de boat comes up de ribbah
    Whistlin' 'roun' de lower bow
I mus' leebe de ole plantation—
    Yas, must say good-bye en go."

Down the Mississippi

Massa so't o' bowed his haid, sah,
    Sittin' in 'is ole-ahm-chair;
Missus, standin' on de do'step
    Caught de sunlight in her hair;
An' de breezes from de orchard
    'Peared to rustle froo de trees,
En I h'yard old Judy weepin'
    Wid de chillun 'roun' her knees.

Tale yo' I was mighty sad, sah,
    But I sort o' walked away.
Years en years ago it was, sah;
    Now I 'se wanderin' back to-day.
'Deed I 'se lookin' back en gazin'
    Mos'ly now each side de stream.
Lan'marks gittin' mighty natch'l,
    'Clar hit 'pears jais like a dream.

Dar 's de place! Dat 's hit, dar, cap'n,
    Dis yere side de ole ho'n bow;
'Low yo' need n't stop de steamah;
    Jais slack up a leetle—slow.
   *   *   *   *   *
Dar 's de same ole steps a-climbin'
    F'om de landin' to de hill.

Down the Mississippi

La n' ob goodness! Ef de bushes
    Ain't a-growin' thickah still.

In de lan' ob de forgotten;
    Not a soul along de hill;
Not a voice to wake yo' gladness;
    Everything do 'pear so still;
Not an echo to a footstep;
    Not an ansah to a call
'Sep' a mockin'-bird a-singin'
    To de lonesomeness—dat 's all.

THE MERMAID

SWEET mermaid of the incomparable eyes,
    Surpassing glimpses of the April skies.
Thy form, ah, maid of the billowy deep!
So rare and fair, but to possess I'd creep
Where the old octopus deep in his briny haunts
Comes forth to feed on anything he wants;
Where mollusks crawl and cuttlefish entwine,
There on crustaceans be content to dine.
What ecstacies in some calcareous valley,
Had I but scales like thee 'tis there we'd dally,
There seek each peak and let no other bliss
Be more enchanting than one salt-sea kiss;
There sit and bask in love, and sigh, and feel
Each other's fins throb, or perhaps we'd steal
To some lone cavern. I suppose you know a
Place where we could pluck the polyzoa,
Or in your boudoir by your mirror there
I'd comb the seaweed from your auburn hair.

The Mermaid

But hush! A red-haired mermaid sister comes this way,
And lashing with her tail the wavelets into spray.
Cometh she alone o'er yonder watery pampas?
Oh, no. By Jove! There comes the white hippocampus.

DE BLACKBIRD FETCHED DE SPRING

WHEN de autumn leabes was twistin'
　　An' a tryin' ter git loose,
An' de apples in de cidah press
　　Had done turned inter juice;
When de blackbird got down-hearted
　　An' made up his mind ter go,
Hit was den de time dis dahky's heart
　　Was jes' pahboiled wid woe.

He was wid me in de furries
　　In de summah fields ob co'n,
An' aroun' a-hookin' cherries—
　　'Deed he was, mos' ebbery mo'n,
An' he he'p me dribe de horses,
　　Cluckt an' cluckt ter make 'em go.
Dat 's why I 'low dis dahky's heart
　　Was jes' pahboiled wid woe.

De Blackbird Fetched De Spring

But he notice dat de yellerin'
 Was a-comin' on de leabes,
An' de win' was so't o' whinin', too,
 Jes' like a dog dat grebes,
An' wid nuffin' in de cherry tree,
 Exceptin' wintah's bref,
One day in fall he 'lowed he 'd go
 En jes' skip out himself.

Hi kain't persarsely blame 'im,
 Kase I 'd went ef I was him;
'Low he knew de wintah wedder
 Would done freeze 'im to de limb,
Kase he could n't ha'dly navigate,
 Er could n't cluck er sing,
En so he said: "Good-bye, ole man,
 I 'se comin' back in spring."

Dis mohnin', honey, 'deed I heerd,
 When ebberyt'ing was calm,
A song dat tetched mah po' ole heart
 Like oil of gladdest balm.
An' who should I see settin' dar
 Upon de ole hay rack,
But mah blackbird, shuah, mah blackbird,
 An' 'e said, "I 'se jes' got back."

De Blackbird Fetched De Spring

Den he opened up his warble,
    When de gentle winds so soft
Came dancin' from de hill-tops dar,
    An' o'er de meddah croft.
An' down hyar by mah cabin do'
    He sang an' flashed his wing,
An' I praised de Lo'd of glory,
    Kase my blackbird fetched de spring.

APPEARANCES

DE man dat wahs de slickest tile
    Doan draw de bigges' check;
De riches' lookin' kin' ob sile
    Doan yiel' de bigges' peck.

De hoss dat 's highes' in de pool
    Doan always win de race,
Kase sometimes he 's a little off,
    An' sometimes held fo' place.

De bulldog wid de orn'ry jaw
    Ain' half so bad to meet
As dat dar yaller mungril cur
    Dat 's layin for yo' meat.

De mooley cow dat hists her leg
    An' makes de milkmaid scream,
Am jes' de bossie cow dat gives
    De riches' kin' ob cream.

De mule dat hab de wicked eye
    Ain' half so bad, now min'—
Look out for dat ole sleepy mule
    Yo' 's walkin' 'roun' behin'.

THE GIRL WITH THE JERSEY

YOU can sing of the maid
    Who, in faultless attire,
Rides out in her curtained coupé;
Her robes are exquisitely fashioned by Worth—
At eve they are décolleté;
But I, I will sing of a maiden more fair,
More innocent, too, I opine;
You can choose from society's crust, if you will,
But the girl with the jersey is mine.

I know her by all that is good, kind and true,
This modest young maiden I name;
I've walked with her, talked with her,
Danced with her, too,
And found that my heart was aflame;
I've written her letters, and small billet-doux,
Revealing my love in each line:
You can drink to your slim, satin-bodiced gazelle,
But the girl with the jersey is mine.

IF MY WIFE TAUGHT SCHOOL

IF I had a wife 'at taught school I would go
To far-away countries. I 'd fish from the Po
In a gondola gay, and the splash o' my oar
Would be heard by the natives around Singapore
   If my wife taught school, .
   I would, would n't you ?
   Er would n't yuh ?
   Enny way, what would you do ?

If I had a wife 'at taught school I would get
Something fine in the shape of a furniture set ;
If I could pay my board and she could pay hern,
There 's a good many nice little things I could earn.
   If my wife taught school,
   I would, would n't you ?
   Er would n't yuh ?
   Enny way, what would you do ?

If my wife taught school you can bet I would fly
Like a condor, I 'd roost pretty middlin' high ;

If My Wife Taught School

I'd wear a silk tile and own hosses, I vow,
And do lots of things I ain't doin' now.
>If my wife taught school,
>I would, would n't you?
>Er would n't yuh?
>Enny way, what would you do?

If my wife taught school like some women do,
And I could n't earn quite enough for us two,
I'd go in the barnyard, without any fuss,
I would blow out my brains with a big blunderbuss.
>If my wife taught school,
>I would, would n't you?
>Er would n't yuh?
>Enny way, what would you do?

THE OLD SPINNING WHEEL

DO you remember the old spinning wheel
That stood in the attic so many years ago,
'Twas covered o'er with dust, and our mother used
    to say
'Twas an old family relic of our grandmother's
    day.
    How the spinning wheel would creak
    As if it tried to speak,
Recalling tender memories of yore ;
    How, back in other years,
    Her eyes would fill with tears
As she heard the hum upon the attic floor.
    Creak, creak, how it would creak,
    When up to the attic we'd steal,
    But mother would say :
    " Boys, come away
From grandmother's old spinning wheel."

Do you remember the cobwebs that clung
To the old oaken beams in the house we were born,

The Old Spinning Wheel

And there from the rafters how memory brings
Back the sage and catnip and the dried apple strings.
    But ah! no other joys
    Compared, when we were boys,
When we played upon the dear old attic floor.
    To slowly turn the wheel—
    And the spindle and the reel
Would sing the dear old song it sang of yore
    Creak, creak, how it would creak,
    When up to the attic we'd steal.
    But mother would say:
    " Boys, come away
From grandmother's old spinning wheel."

THE OWL AND THE CROW

THERE was an old owl,
  With eyes big and bright,
Who sung in a treetop
  One calm summer night.
And the song that he sung
  I will now sing to you—
" To whit ! To whoo, hoo !
  To whit ! To whoo, hoo !"

He sang there all night
  Till early next morn,
When a crow came along
  That was looking for corn.
The crow heard him singing,
  " To whit ! To whoo, hoo !"
And offered to sing
  A few notes that he knew.

Just then the old owl
  In the treetop so high,

The Owl and the Crow

With his classical shape
   And his big staring eye,
Requested the crow,
   In the deepest of scorn,
To sing his old chestnut
   About stealing corn.

" Caw! Caw! " said the crow,
   " Well—my deeds are by light.
I do n't steal young chickens
   And sit up all night,
With dew on my feathers;
   When I break the laws
In looking through cornfields
   It 's not without caws "

DE CLOUDS AM GWINE TER PASS

DE wedder's mighty waum,
An' I gase it's gwine ter staum,
Doan yo' see de swaller flyin' to de thatch?
Black clouds a-sweepin' by,
Jes' a-skimmin' long de sky,
Dar's a-hustlin' in de huckleberry patch.

Dar's Zeke and Hezekiah,
Jane Ann an' ole Maria,
Mighty skeery when dey see de lightnin' flash.
How dey hustle to de cabin,
Whar ole Dinah am a-blabbin'
An de hoe cake am a-bakin' in de ash.

I tole yo' kase I know,
Jes' what make it thundah so,
Dat's de way Gord shake de rain out ob de sky;
An' when yo' hyar de soun'
Like a shubbin' tables roun'
Yo' can see de pigs a-runnin' to de sty.

De Clouds Am Gwine Ter Pass

    But de clouds am gwine ter pass,
      An' de sun shine out at las',
While de pickaninnies play aroun' de do';
      An' froo de windah blinds,
      Hid by mornin' glory vines,
Hit 's er gwine to flicker down upon de flo'.

      Gord moves in many a way,
      So de ole Bible say,
Fo' He counts de drops and all de grains ob san';
      An' when de darkness falls
      'Pon dese hyar cabin walls
Hit am jes' de break ob day in uddah lands.

Den hurry, chillun, hustle while you may,
Kase yo' know dar 's gwine ter come a rainy day.
      But de gloomerin' will pass,
      An' de sun shine out at las',
An' de darkies' clouds ob sorrer pass away.

A SUMMER'S AFTERNOON

'TWAS the close of a summer's day,
  The sound of the flail had died away,
The sun was shedding a lingering gleam,
And the teakettle sung with its load of steam.
The old clock ticked that hung on the wall
And struck 'ith the same old cuckoo call;
Then oft I could hear the mournful bay
Of some watch-dog far away.
Then all ter onct piped in a jay.
I just sot there with my senses gone,
And the shadders of twilight a-creepin' on,
With the eerie hum of the small pee-wees,
Over there in the cedar trees,
And the tinkle of bells in the marshy loam
'At told me the cows were coming home,
And the sighing breeze came o'er the croft,
But ah! comes a melody far more soft
Than the troubled notes of a lydian lute
Or the echoing strains of a fairy's flute;

A Summer's Afternoon

It bids me awaken and live and rejoice,
'Tis only the sound of Elviry's voice—
Like an angel's whisper it comes to me :—
"Wake up, you fool, and come to tea."
An' it ain't in the spring er it ain't in the fall,
But the close of a summer's day,
                    That's all.

I FED THE FISHES

ONE day a big excursion sailed afar out in the lake,
All bent upon an outing with their sandwiches and cake.
They sought the upper deck until the wind began to blow,
When all engaged in different things as every one must know;
>While I fed the fishes,
>I fed the fishes,

I fed the fishes clear to Old St. Joe.

Good Captain Stines went up on deck to cast his weather eye;
A woman sadly, badly prayed, "Oh, Father, let me die!"
The cabin-boys ran back and forth in staterooms all around,
While voices shrieked: "Oh, mercy—oop! Oh—oop! wish I were drowned."

I Fed the Fishes

    But I fed the fishes,
    I gave them my best wishes,
I fed the fishes clear to Old St. Joe.

The pilot boldly held the wheel as through the waves we sped,
While Purser Hancock ran abaft to hold some woman's head;
One fellow sat him down and sang: "Good-bye, sweetheart, good-bye;"
Most every one seemed occupied, and, sad to say, then I—
    I fed the fishes,
    I fed the fishes,
I fed the fishes clear to Old St. Joe.

The "Chicora" rose up in the air and then came down "kersock;"
She wibble-wobbled in the sea and once she struck a rock;
The purser wore a pallid look, the women all turned pale,
While calmly I sat out on deck and hung over the rail;
    For I fed the fishes,
    I gave them my best wishes,
I fed the fishes clear to Old St. Joe.

I Fed the Fishes

Some tried to eat their sandwiches, some staggered, reeled and laughed,
While others went below to smile, and there the brown ale quaffed.
The steward, Richard Waters, rushed about with whisky slings;
Most every one seemed occupied, and all did different things,
        But I fed the fishes,
        I fed the fishes,
I fed the fishes clear to Old St. Joe.

OLD BOSSIE COW

PO' ole bossie cow 's down in de marsh,
  Down in de marsh where de col' winds am blowin',
Eb'ry now an' den when de staum dies away
Seems if I hyard ole bossie cow a-lowin'.

So out by de cabin do' I stan' on de sweep,
An' listen in de win' an' dampnin' weddah,
An 't 'pears dat I hear ole bossie cow agin,
An' I low dat she say, "Come down in de meddah."

Den down froo de marsh land trampin' along,
Down froo de gloom an' de night rains a-fallin',
Pickin' my way through the whisperin' reeds,
"Co-boss, co-boss, co-boss" a-callin'.

Den all ob a sudden I come to a stop,
An' dar ole bossie cow so gentle an' so kyind;
An' I coax up ole brindle, an' I lead her by de ho'n;
A wee little bossie cow comes follerin' on behin',
A wee little bossie comes follerin' on behin'.

THAT CAT

THE cat that comes to my window sill
When the moon looks cold and the night is still—
He comes in a frenzied state alone
With a tail that stands like a pine tree cone,
And says : "I have finished my evening lark,
And I think I can hear a hound dog bark.
My whiskers are froze 'nd stuck to my chin.
I do wish you'd git up and let me in."
   That cat gits in.

But if in the solitude of the night
He does n't appear to be feeling right,
And rises and stretches and seeks the floor,
And some remote corner he would explore,
And does n't feel satisfied just because
There's no good spot for to sharpen his claws,
And meows and canters uneasy about
Beyond the least shadow of any doubt
   That cat gits out.

A FROG'S THANKSGIVING

I'M a frog with a shanty built over each eye,
   And a terrible push when I get on a hump;
There's very few reptiles that's one-half so spry
Or can come up along side o' me on the jump.

I'm a frog when the other birds take to the wing
And wander away beneath balmier skies;
I belong to the bloated batrachian ring
With a pneumatic palate for coaxing in flies.

I'm a frog in the fall and a frog when the frost
Spreads over the land, and the forests are gray.
I'm a frog keepin' house at a very small cost
In a dug-out I've built out o' cat-tails and clay.

I'm a frog with a green overcoat and a voice
That tickles the woods, when the winter's no more.
The old folks are glad and children rejoice,
At the first tap o' thunder, I let out a roar.

I'm a frog living down in the lush of the swale;
You all know my voice when I'm looting for game.
They call me a cannibal—what a sad tale.
Well, maybe I am; I'm a frog just the same.

LOVEY-LOVES

OH, love! let us love with a love that loves,
    Loving on with a love forever;
For a love that loves not the love it should love—
    I wot such a love will sever.
But, when two loves love this lovable love,
    Love loves with a love that is best;
And this love-loving, lovable, love-lasting love
    Loves on in pure love's loveliness.

Oh, chide not the love when its lovey-love loves
    With lovable, loving caresses;
For one feels that the lovingest love love can love,
    Loves on in love's own lovelinesses.
And love, when it does love, in secret should love—
    'Tis there where love most is admired;
But the two lovey-loves that do n't care where they love
    Make the public most mightily tired.

HANK SPINK

HANK SPINK, he said—er Bob did, his brother—
'At he hit a man once for somepin or other,
An' after he hit 'im—I got this from Bob—
He simply went right out an' give up his job;
Not Hank er Bob,
    But the feller 'at got hit
Give up his job.
        See?

He said 'at the wind, er the force of his blow,
Er somepin like that, somehow—I do n't know
Just now what it was—I got it from Bob,
'At he got a good swat; not Hank er Bob,
By a long shot,
    But the feller 'at got hit
Got a good swat.
        See?

He said he 'd be blamed, 'at he did n't know
How he came to strike such an all-fired blow,

Hank Spink

'Cept he guarded his right an' threw the hull heft
Of his weight an' his science, an' hit with his left ;
That lost 'im his job ; not Hank er Bob,
    But the feller 'at got hit,
Lost him his job.
              See ?

THE NILE

NOT a single cloud bedims the sky,
   Not a shadow falls below,
But crocodiles creep, enfeebled by heat,
   Through the lotus flowers that grow
On the banks of the Nile, the placid Nile,
   The Nile of ages ago.

So sluggish and wan it wanders on
   Where the citron and doum palms grow,
Where Sphinxes stare, through the lurid air,
   At the sun in its molten glow ;
That's called the Nile, the tranquil Nile,
   Of ages and ages ago.

On the purple sheen of its mirror heart
   Her galleys bend and row,
And Egypt's queen can still be seen,
   Of olden lands the foe.
Ah ! this was the Nile, the ancient Nile,
   The Nile of the long ago.

The Nile

By ashen banks of the ancient stream
   The acacia tree bends low,
The ibis stands in this tomb of lands,
   As if in a pallor of woe,
On the banks of the Nile, the sacred Nile,
   The Nile of ages ago.

LIKE DE OLE MULE BES'

SOME folks is so't o' pa'shal to de cattle roun' de fa'm,
Ter make a pet ob animals dey find hit so't of balm,
While odders 'fer de poultry stock; de goose, en duck, en hen
Is often made de mos' ob by de wisess kind ob men.
Some like de brindle mooley cow 'nd 'low dey hab de sense
Ter pear ter know dere massa we'n dey see 'im at de fence.
Some like the yearlin' colt; I've raly seed men stand aroun'
An' pet a hoss all day, 'nd rub his legs en fetlocks down;
But gibbin all de animals de faires' kind ob tes'
    I so't o' like de ole mule bes'.

Some pet de mockin' bird en robin redbress' an' de linnit;
Some like de gobbler kase he's struttin' roun' mos' ebery minute.

Like De Ole Mule Bes'

Some like de peacock fo' his pride, an' den some like de dog,
Whilst odders fo companionship have prefunce fo' de hog.
Some fa'mers like de wedder sheep, en some de little lam',
De billy-goat, an' nanny-goat, whilst odders 'fer de ram.
Some like de little week-ol' calf w'en buntin' roun' hits mudder,
An' some folks dey like one thing an' den some folks like anudder;
But 'f all de stock I'se raised wid in de Souf, er Eas' er Wes'
    I so't o' like de ole mule bes'.

Dars sompin' meekly 'bout 'im, hits de fac' he is n't bold
An' de 'spression on 'is face is like de holy saints ob old;
When he sort o' histe 'is heel up like 's gwine ter hit de sky
He 's simply exahcisin' jes ter pestervate a fly.
An' de why he 'pears embarrass'd is kase nature had ter fail

Like De Ole Mule Bes'

An' made 'im sort o' long on ears, en kind o' short on tail;
But den he's mo den 'tatched ter me, and know I is his frien'
An' we done made up our mind ter stick tergedder ter de end;
So dar's no use ob yo' axin' me, yo's done had time ter guess
    I so't o' like de ole mule bes'.

I used ter like Lucindy, but den 'Cindy could n't stay,
An' little Sim, I worshiped so, de angels coaxed away,
An' Lize Anne, an' br'er Zeph dere up dar on de hill,
I pa'shley think I hear 'em, too, w'en all aroun' is still;
Yo' see I'se mo' den lonesome heah, wid nobody ter talk,
Er hide behin' de lilac trees adown de garden walk,
Dat w'en I look at dat ole mule I feel so full ob woe
'Bout little Sim 'at rode on 'im, an 'taint so long ago,
Ob all de frien's dat's lef' me now, I 'raly mus' confess
    I so't o' like de ole mule bes'.

DE RIBBER OB LIFE

I DREAMT dat I saw de ribber ob life
    Dat flows to de Jaspah Sea.
De angels war wadin' to an' fro,
    But none ob 'em spoke to me.
Some dipped dere wings in de silb'ry tide;
Some war alone an' some side by side.
Nary a one dat I knew could I see
    In dat ribber ob life,
      De ribber ob life
    Dat flows to de Jaspah Sea.

De ribber was wide, dat ribber ob life;
    De bottom I plainly could see.
De stones layin' dar was whiter dan snow;
    De sands looked like gold to me.
De angels kep' wadin' to an' fro;
Whar did dey come from?
Whar did dey go?
None ob 'em sinnahs like me, I kno',

De Ribber Ob Life

    In dat ribber ob life,
    De ribber ob life
Dat flows to de Jaspah Sea.

De watah was clear as de "well by de gate,"
    Whar Jesus de light first see.
De sofes' ob music f'om angel bands
Come ober dat ribber ob golden sands,
    Come ober dat ribber to me.
An' den I saw de clouds break away,
Revealin' de pearly gates ob day,
De beautiful day dat nebber shall cease,
Where all is joy, an' lub, an' peace.
An' ovah dem gates was written so clear:
"Peace to all who entah here."
De angels was gedderin' 'roun' de frone,
De gates done closed, I was lef' alone,
Alone on de banks ob a darkenin' stream,
But when I awoke I foun' 'twas a dream.

I 'se gwine to ford dat ribber ob life
    An' see de eternal day.
I 'se gwine to hear dem heavenly bands,
An' feel de tech ob ole-time hands
    Dat long hab passed away.
Dar 's crowns ob glory for all, I 'm told,

De Ribber Ob Life

An' lubly harps wid strings ob gold.
An' I know ef dar 's peace beyond dat sea,
Wid res' fo' de weary, dar 's res' fo' me --
Beyond dat ribber, dat ribber ob life,
    Dat flows to de Jaspah Sea.

THE CAT O' NINE TAILS

THE old cat o' nine tails is comin' 'round agin,
   And the way he worries children sometimes is a sin ;
He grabs 'em by the collar, an' he yanks 'em by the clothes
And reaches for a tender place. Why, what do you suppose
Will happen if you 're impident an' set aroun' an' grin ?
Well, I 'll have to call the cat o' nine tails in—
Have to call him in ; yes, have to call him in ;
                                  in.
                          tails
                  cat o' nine
            old
I 'll have to call the old cat o' nine tails in.
            old
                  cat o' nine
                          tails
                                  in.

The Cat O' Nine Tails

Are you sassy to yer father, are you fibbin' to yer mother?
Are you quarrelin' with yer sister an' a-pinchin' of yer brother,
Do you "ring around the rosey" till you have a dizzy feelin',
And you think yer goin' 'roun' an' 'roun' an' walkin' on the ceilin'?
Well, you better stop yer screechin' an' a-makin' such a din,
Er I'll have to call the old cat o' nine tails in—
Have to call him in; yes, have to call him in;
                              in.
                         tails
                    cat o' nine
               old
I'll have to call the old cat o' nine tails in.
               old
                    cat o' nine
                         tails
                              in.

Do you allers mind your manners when company is come?
Er do you git upstairs 'nd yell, 'nd stomp around 'nd drum?

The Cat O' Nine Tails

Do you show off at the table, too, 'nd try to act up smart,
'Nd p'int yer fingers at the things 'nd say : "Gimme a tart ?"
If some one doesn't dress you down I think it is a sin ;
So I'll have to call the old cat o' nine tails in—
Have to call 'im in ; yes, have to call 'im in ;
                                in.
                        tails
                cat o' nine
            old
I'll have to call the old cat o' nine tails in.
            old
                cat o' nine
                        tails
                                in.

THE HAIR-TONIC BOTTLE

HOW dear to my heart is the old village drug-
store,
When tired and thirsty it comes to my view.
The wide-spreading sign that asks you to "Try it,"
Vim, Vaseline, Vermifuge, Hop Bitters, too.
The old rusty stove and the cuspidor by it,
That little back room. Oh! you've been there
yourself,
And ofttimes have gone for the doctor's prescription,
But tackled the bottle that stood on the shelf.
      The friendly old bottle,
      The plain-labeled bottle,
The "Hair-Tonic" bottle that stood on the shelf.

How oft have I seized it with hands that were glowing,
And guzzled awhile ere I set off for home;
I owned the whole earth all that night, but next
morning
My head felt as big as the Capitol's dome.

The Hair-Tonic Bottle

And then how I hurried away to receive it,
   The druggist would smile o'er his poisonous pelf,
And laugh as he poured out his unlicensed bitters,
   And filled up the bottle that stood on the shelf.
      The unlicensed bottle,
      The plain-labeled bottle,
That "Hair-Tonic" bottle that stood on the shelf.

DE CIRCUS TURKEY

HE'S de worst I evah see,
    Dat old turkey up 'n de tree,
I bin pesta'n him 'n punchin' him saince mohnin'.
    I nev' saince I was bo'n
    See de way he do stick on,
En he 'pears to look down at me 's if he scornin'.

    He does n't seem to 'pear
    Ter hab a bit ob fear,
Kase I 'se wasted all mah strength 'n bref upon 'im.
    It may be he 's in fun,
    But I 'll scah 'im wid dis gun,
I 'se boun' ter git 'im down some way, dog on 'im.

    I 'se fro'd mos' all de sticks
    In de yard, 'n all de bricks;
Ef yo' was me whut under d' sun 'ud yo' do?
    He does n't seem ter change,
    'N' 'pears ter act so strange,
I d'clar he mus' be pestah'd wid a hoodoo.

De Circus Turkey

       I tale yo' hit 's er fac'
       I nearly broke mah back
Er histin' shoes 'n brickbats up dar to 'im
       'Pon dis Tanksgibbin' day.
       I hate ter shoot, but say—
I bleebe a gun 's de only thing 'll do 'im.

       I 'low I 'll make 'im think
       He kaint gib me de wink
An' sait upon dat limb en be secuah.
       Biff!—! Bang!—! I 'll make 'im sing;
       Mah goodness, watch 'im swing.
W'y he 's a reg'lah circus turkey, suah.

       Hi see de hull thing now—
       Dat Rasmus boy, I 'low,
Has done gone tied 'is feet up dar wid strings.
       No wondah dat he tried
       Ter come off; he was tied
'N' all what he could do was flap 'is wings.

       Come hyar, yo' Rasmus, quick, sah!
       I 'se min' ter use dis stick, sah!
Come hyar, from ovah dar, from whar yo' stood.
       I 'low I ought to lay yo'
       Down on dat groun' en flay yo'
I 'se tempted mos' ter use a stick o' wood.

De Circus Turkey

Yo' kaint go de meetin',
An' w'en it comes ter eatin'
Yo' mudder sais yo' kaint come to de table.
I bet yo 'll sing er tune,
Kase all dis aftahnoon
We 's 'cided dat we 'll lock yo' in de stable.

Yo' kaint hab none de white meat,
An' yo' kaint hab none de brown meat,
An' yo' jes' hearn whut yer po' ole mudder sade;
Yo' kaint hab none de stuffin'
Er de cranber' sauce er nuffin',
An' 'cisely at six o'clock yo' go ter baid.

SOFIE JAKOBOWSKI

LITTLE Sofie Jakobowski,
Handsome as a forest flower,
Dwelt alone with Gokstad Pfouski
Ivan Ruric Romanowski,
In the palace of the tower,
Of the ancient tower of Ivan,
Dwelt she in the long ago,
Near by where the frozen Volga
Sleeps beneath its weight of snow.

Now, it seems old Gokstad Pfouski
Ivan Ruric Romanowski
Had a passion for the maid,
And was very much afraid
That perhaps she might get frisky—
Fall in love with John Zobiesky;
So he locked her in the tower
Oft for many a weary hour.
He, the old decrepit sinner,

Sofie Jakobowski

Kept her locked up growing thinner,
Many a week and month she staid
In that tower, and often laid
Down to rest upon the cold
Marble floor, so I am told
By an old Slavonic story
That is gray and bald and hoary;
'Tis a legend that's so weird
Soft winds gently comb its beard.
Little Sofie Jakobowski
Was the fairest of the fair;
Eyes that seemed half way confessing,
Yet would keep you coldly guessing,
Hair that in each wavy fold
Tales of witchery unrolled—
Being that old Angelo
Traced in cloisters long ago;
Lips, those liquid lips who dew
Is tinctured with the rose's hue;
Cheeks afire with the glow
Of maidenhood; a neck of snow.
Hoping, grieving, sighing, praying
For her lover, disobeying
When she dared old Gokstad Pfouski
Ivan Ruric Romanowski,

Sofie Jakobowski

Even hoping to the end
For her little Polish friend.
Now it might be said if any
Maid had lovers she had many ;
Old traditions name a score.
Put perhaps a dozen more
On the little maiden's list,
For her charms who could resist ?
She could bring them from Siberia,
Hindostan, or far-off Syria,
From the Deutscher Zuyder Zee
To the rat-rice-fed Chinee.
There was little Moses Khan
From the village of Kasan,
Vadlimir, and Max Pulaski,
Peter Ulrich, and Hydrasky,
Isaac Ozam of Torique,
One Jim Bogado, a Greek,
And a soldier, Peter Hensky,
Of the noted Prebojenski ;
Kutusoff and Fedorovitch,
Little No Account von Storitch,
Seizendorf, and Jake Zebatzki,
Romanoff and Ruffonratzsky,
This is but the half of them—

Sofie Jakobowski

Herr von Freitag Stobelpem,
And a Jew that sent her Rhine wine,
Moses Aaron Eiffel Einstein;
He from Hong Kong, Sam Wing Lee,
Drinkee Allee Samee Tea;
Isawwiskey and Tschenimsky,
Waronetski and Chewbimsky,
And two nase a yentlemen,
Yohn and Ole Petersen.

She could bring them, I presume,
From the far-off land of doom,
Each with one intent to woo her,
Ardent, doing homage to her,
Sending presents from Australia,
Nuggets from the Himalaya
Mountains, rings and souvenirs
Enough to last a hundred years;
Arrows almost every hour
Carried presents to the tower.
Do n't you think it quite a sin
They had to shoot their presents in?
Think of how a despot's power
Kept her locked up in a tower.
She the fairest little maiden

Sofie Jakobowski

Dwelling on this side of Aidin;
Would n't any lover plunge in
To the deepest Russian dungeon,
Or become a serf and work
Out his life at Nedjikerk
To kidnap from yonder tower
That sweet little Russian flower?
So I would, so did the frisky
Nihilist, young John Zobiesky.
Now the father of Zobiesky
Manufactured awful whisky,
But young John took more delight
In making bombs and dynamite,
And he entertained the Russians
With a series of concussions
Till they wanted him so bad
That it made all Russia sad.
Once I think he came not far
From blowing up " the only " czar,
But he had a most surprising
Way of hiding and disguising—
Never man as yet had found him,
Never army could surround him.
Probably he had a mascot—
Born a regular Russian Tascott.

Sofie Jakobowski

John Zobiesky seemed contented
When he had them all fermented
'Round the palace.   Near the gate
Cossack soldiers stood up straight,
Guarding with their guns and sabers
One another from their neighbors ;
Over there one can't resist
The thought to praise the nihilist.
Every day and every hour
You feel the despot's potent power ;
Every day you want to shoot
Some old potentate and scoot ;
So with John.   One day he saw
Another way to break the law.
Listen !   John was discontented,
And his smart brain soon invented
With saltpeter and corrosives
Something awful in explosives.
Then with heart chuck full, elated,
Little John sat down and waited—
Waited for the somber curtain
Of the night to make him certain
That he might not be discovered
Or his hellish plans uncovered,
Waited till a cloudy pall

Sofie Jakobowski

Hung its mantle over all,
And Stygian darkness reigning far
Hid each peeping, tell-tale star,
That lately had begun to nod
From Omsk to Nijni-Novgorod.
Then he stole up to that tower,
Just beneath his lady's bower.
Fearlessly he placed enough
Of that paralyzing stuff
In the chinks and the foundation
Of that tower to blast a nation.
Then he sat him down and wrote
Forty letters—make a note.
He wrote forty, understand,
Wrote them in a woman's hand.
" I love only—only you ;
Come to-night, sweet love.   Adieu ! "
Signing with a heart aflame,
Sofie Jakobowski's name.

One dark night when all was still
On frosty turret, dome and hill,
Forty suitors came in season,
Knocked, and—I do n't know the reason—
Walked right in the door ; it swung

Sofie Jakobowski

Open, then it closed and sprung;
Every lover seemed to fare
The same, for they were prisoners there
They were in beyond a doubt,
With no chance of getting out.
Now the risky John Zobiesky
Had the Cossacks drunk on whisky,
And guards with their long sabers,
Rested sweetly from their labors.
Sofie Jakobowski, frisky,
Looked down on her John Zobiesky;
John Zobiesky gazed at Sofie
And he longed to gain the trophy.
Sofie, up there in the casement,
Throwing kisses towards the basement—
John Zobiesky at the basement
Hurling kisses to the casement.
But he has no time to lose;
Fixing up that deadly fuse,
Now he hurls a line up till
It reaches Sofie's window sill.
Scarcely had she made it fast
When the maiden stood aghast!
Startled at what stood before her—
John Zobiesky, her adorer.

Sofie Jakobowski

Do n't get anxious ; I must own
John and Sofie were alone.
And I know a Russian kiss
Is not such hard-frozen bliss.
'Twas the first in years that they
Had thus embraced—the time that way—
So they occupied the present
Till the night had grown senescent ;
And they wondered oft how fared
The lovers down below that shared
The palace of old Gokstad Pfouski
Ivan Ruric Romanowski.

" Hark ! " cried Sofie, " 't is the hour
When Moscow's bell in yonder tower
Peals a knell, and we must fly,
Or else together we must die.
Ah, look ! through yonder gate I see
That demon—and he comes to me—
The wretch that locks and keeps me here
From month to month and year to year."
Up jumps the risky little frisky
Nihilist, young John Zobiesky.
A kiss upon her lips, his hand
Upon his breast as if to brand

Sofie Jakobowski

His vow : "You say, 'He comes to me ;'
You cry : 'He comes ! He comes ! To thee
I swear by yonder moonlit snow
He comes !' Just watch and see him go."
Then with Sofie on his shoulder—
Never fear that he can't hold her—
Through the window, down the rope,
The nihilist and maid elope.
Not a moment do they lose,
Save to stop and light the fuse.
Slowly on its path it crawls
Toward the gray old castle walls,
Past the Cossacks with their sabers,
Still at rest from recent labors,
And the noble body guard—
They are snoring just as hard.
A flash ! A roar ! and Moscow rumbles,
And the tower of Ivan tumbles.
Up skyhigh went Godstad Pfouski
Ivan Ruric Romanowski,
Also little Moses Khan
Of the village of Kazan ;
Vadlimir and Max Pulaski,
Peter Ulric, and Hydraski ;
Isaac Ozam of Torique,

Sofie Jakobowski

One Jim Bogado, a Greek,
And a soldier, Peter Henski,
Of the noted Prebojenski ;
Kutuseff and Fedorovitch,
Little No Account von Stovitch,
Seizendorf and Jake Zebatzski,
Remanoff and Ruffonratzski,
This is but the half of them,
Herr von Freitag Stobelpem
And a Jew that sent her Rhine wine,
Moses Aaron Eiffel Einstein,
Drinkee Allee Samee Tea—
He from Hong Kong—Sam Wing Lee,
Isawwiskey and Tschenimsky,
Waronetzski and Chewbimsky,
And two nase a yentlemen,
Yohn and Ole Petersen.

SUNRISE

THE dim light to the sou'ward
    Is the beacon of the coast,
But the white light to the leeward
    The mariner loves most.
And whether 'tis the dim light
    Or the white light to the lee,
That great big hunk of daylight
    Is light of lights for me.
But what it is of all lights
    That fills my soul with glee,
Is when that hunk of daylight
    Climbs up out of the sea.

THE WOODTICKS

THERE'S things out in the forest
    That's worser an' 'n owl,
'At gets on naughty boys 'n girls
    'At allers wears a scowl.
There's things out in the forest
    'At's worser 'n a lion,
'At gets on wicked boys 'n girls
    'At's quarrelin' an' a-cryin'.
There's things out in the forest, mind,
    An' if you do n't take care,
The woodticks—the woodticks—
    Will be crawlin' thro' yer hair.

An' they say as boys is naughty,
    An' their hearts is full o' sin,
They'll crawl out in the night time
    An' get underneath yer skin,
An' the doctor'll have to take a knife
    An' cut 'em off jes' so,

The Woodticks

An' if a bit of 'em is left
    Another one 'll grow.
An' mebbe you won't feel 'em, too,
    Er ever know they're there,
But by and by they'll multiply
    And crawl up in yer hair.

The devil's darnin' needle too,
    'Ill come and sew yer ear.
An' make a nest inside like that,
    An' then you'll never hear;
An' the jigger bugs gets on you,
    An the thousand-legged worm
'Ill make you writhe, an' twist, an' groan,
    An' cry, an' yell, an' squirm;
But the worst things 'at 'll git you
    If you lie, or steal, or swear,
Is the woodticks—the woodticks—
    A-crawlin' thro' yer hair.

DIDN'T WE, JIM?

YES, sir; we lived home till our mother died,
    An' I'd go a-walkin' with Jim, cause he cried,
Till night time 'ud come, 'nd we'd go up to bed
An' bofe say the prayers 'at she taught us ter said—
        Didn't we, Jim?

An' pa 'ud stay late, an' we uster call,
'Cause we thought we heard 'im downstairs in the hall:
An' when he come home once he fell on the floor,
An' we run'd an' hid behind ma's bedroom door—
        Didn't we, Jim?

She told us, our ma did, when she's sick in bed,
An' out of the Bible some verses read,
To never touch wine, and some more I can't think;
But the last words she said was never to drink—
        Didn't she, Jim?

But our other ma, what our pa brought home there,
She whipped little Jim 'cause he stood on a chair

Did n't We, Jim?

An' kissed our ma's picture that hung on the wall,
An' struck me fer not doin' nothin' at all—
    Did n't she, Jim?

She said 'at we never had no bringin' up,
An' stayed 'round the house an' eat everything up,
An' said 'at we could n't have no more to eat,
An' all 'at we 's fit for was out in the street—
    Did n't she, Jim?

We said 'at we hated her, did n't we, Jim?
But our pa—well, we did n't say nothin' ter him,
But just took ma's picture and bofe run'd away;
An' that 's what Jim's cryin' 'bout out here to-day—
    Did n't we, ain't it, Jim?

Mister, do n't feel bad—'cause Jim's cryin'—too;
Fer we 're goin' ter hunt an' git somethin' ter do;
'Cause our ma 'at died said ter work an' ter pray,
An' we 'd all be together in glory some day—
    Did n't she, Jim?

THE POST-DRIVER

THE lingering loon flies over the marsh
    And the night bird nestles in dew,
The river is cold and the winds are harsh,
    But what is it that goes cuhchoo?
    What is it that goes cuhchoo, cuhchoo?
    Oh, what is it that goes cuhchoo?

Then the rail comes up from his lushy bed
    And wings to the realms of blue;
Wild lilies soak where the bullfrogs croak,
    But what is it that goes cuhchoo?
    What is it that goes cuhchoo, cuhchoo?
    Oh, what is it that goes cuhchoo?

O'er the whispering reeds the rice-hen speeds,
    And the meadow-lark singing anew,
And I know in the swail the song of the rail,
    But what is it that goes cuhchoo?
    What is it that goes cuhchoo, cuhchoo?
    Oh, what is it that goes cuhchoo?

LEF' DE OLE HOSS OUT

'TWEEN de gusts ob de win'
    Comes a winner an' a soun'
Like de trampin' ob hoofs on de col', col' groun'.
    I 'se 'spicious ob a staum,
    An' dere ain't no doubt
But somebody 's gone an' lef' de ole hoss out.

    I 'membah now de sheep
    Come a-runnin' to de shed,
An' de ole bossie cow was a-standin' in 'er bed,
    An' de chickens on de roos';
    But what was I 'bout
When I done went to bed an' lef' de ole hoss out?

    Well, I mus'n lay heah
    An' hab de col' win's blow—
When de keyhole whistles dar 's gwine ter come snow—
    I jes' oughter 'rise
    An' wandah right out,
An' cuah myself ob leebin' de ole hoss out.

Lef' De Ole Hoss Out

Mah goodness, what er night!
Wondah what's dat soun'?
Dat's de ole hoss, jes' comin' on de boun'.
I 'se ashame' ob myse'f!
Well, what was I 'bout,
Ter go ter bed ter res' an' leebe de ole hoss out?

EC-A-LEC-TIC FITS

I 'M only jes' a little chap,
   An' my ma says I 'm frail;
I got ec-a-lec-tic fits,
   'At 's why I 'm lookin' pale.
Once I had a ague chill,
   An', oh, how I did shake
'Cause aunty would n't give me any
   Jelly tarts an' cake!

Once when it was summer
   Once, an' nice an' warm, nen me
An' Jennie went in our back yard
   'Nd climbed a cherry tree.
An' she ate all the cherries, too,
   An' fed me all the pits,
An' my ma said 'at 's jes' what give
   Me ec-a-lec-tic fits.

When bad girls comes to our house
   They must n't scare me, too,

Ec-a-lec-tic Fits

An' romp up quick against me
    Like they 's playin' peek-a-boo,
'Cause ma she 'll say right out to 'em:
    "See here, now, children, quit!
I guess you 'll have to run right home
    'Fore Wadsworth has a fit."

Sometime I 'll be strong' nd well
    An' big like Uncle Dan,
An' he 'll be little jes' like me,
    When I 'm a grown-up man,
'Nd nen I won't be scarin' people
    Almost out their wits,
'Cause 'en I won't go 'round a-havin'
    Ec-a-lec-tic fits.

When you see me turnin' blue
    An' when my hands gits cold,
Do n't you git afraid o' that;
    But jes' you git a hold
Of me, an' rub my hands,
    'Nd rub my neck 'nd head
Till I "come out"—'cause if you do n't
    I 'm li'ble to git dead.

I would n't care if I should die
    'Nd go up there, would you,

Ec-a-lec-tic Fits

Where the sun is peekin' 'round
    The clouds, up where it 's blue?
'Cause there they ain't no worry,
    An' they 's lots o' little bits
Of fellers, an' they 's none of 'em
    Got ec-a-lec-tic fits.

KEEP HIM A BABY

KEEP him a baby as long as you can;
    Bless him, the dear little, cute, cunning man!
Keep him in dresses, and apron, and bib;
Rock him to sleep in his own little crib.

Keep him a baby enjoying his toys—
Soon enough he will be one of the boys;
Keep him a baby and keep him at home—
Manhood will very soon cause him to roam.

Ofttimes at night when he wakes for a frolic,
Do n't get excited—it 's only the colic;
When he has reason your slumbers to mar,
Get up and walk with him, just as you are.

First it is Winslow and then it is squills,
Then you will find one or two doctor's bills,
Though he 's a trouble at times, it is true,
When he grows up he will take care of you.

Keep him a baby still taking his nap,
Do n't you chastise him for any mishap;

Keep Him a Baby

When he falls off a sofa or chair,
Do n't stop his crying by calling a bear.

Keep him a baby and do as I say;
Take him to ride in his carriage each day;
Show him the bossie, the horse and the bow-wow;
Soon you will hear him say "moo!" to the cow.

Keep him a baby: he 'll soon be a boy,
Then he 'll forsake every plaything and toy;
Keep him a baby—he 'll soon be a man,
Keep him a baby as long as you can.

ANGELINY

COME right hyar, yo' Angeliny;
    Chile, yo' jes' gib me de blues.
What yo' doin'? tryin' to try me
    Warin' out dem bran new shoes?
Yase yo' is, 'deed yo' is,
    Doan yo' dar talk back to me,
Kase I know yo' is.

Whar' yo' gwine to play dis tennis?
    Who yo' playin' tennis wid;
Playin' wid dat Irish Dennis,
    Well fo' yo,' chile, dat yo's hid.
Come right squar out f'om dar,
    Out f'om dar hin' dat dar bed;
Now, go comb yo' har.

Angeliny! Angeliny!
    Doan yo' hyar me callin' yo'?
Need n't tink dat yo' slip by me,
    Min', gal, I 'se daid on tah yo'.

Angeliny

Come right squar in t'om dar,
  Yo' kaint play wid dem low white trash,
Now, my gal, see hyar.

  Whar's yo' music edgecashun ?
Git to dat piannah dar
Play dat lubly strabaganzah
  Dat yo' calls de Maiden's Pra'r.
Lan' a-libin', chile, do yo'
  Want de folks in dis hyar neighbo'hood
Tink yo 's Irish too ?

DE EYARFQUAKE

DE eyarfquake a-shakin'
    Jes' a short time ago
Was Belzabub a-pullin'
   Out de clinkers down below.
So yo' bettah drap yo' sinnin',
Kase ol' Satan he 's a-grinnin',
Bime-by de big saxafhone
   Am shuahly gwine to blow.

Cose yo 's laffin now,
   Bekase it 's mighty still.
Bime-by she gwine ter shake
   Wid a pow'ful heavy chill;
An' de ole bell in de towah
'S gwine to fall down wid de powah,
An' de millstones go dancin'
   Roun' de bottom ob de mill.

Some day dar 's gwine ter open
   De bigges' kin' ob crack,

The Eyarfquake

An' dis hyar coon 's a-hopin'
　　Dat de Lord won't hol' yo' back,
'Speshly Jaspah Jones McClellan,
'Yo 's de one I 'se bin a-tellin'
'But de use of bad profanity
　　An' also plug terbac.

'Fore de debbil shake
　　De furnace down agin,
Yo' bettah ask de Lord
　　To rid yo' ob yo' sin,
Kase when Satan wants some fuel
To warm up his brimstone gruel
He 'll ope de furnace do'
　　An' de draf' 'll suck yo' in.

Doan be loafin' now
　　An' shootin' craps aroun';
Yo' bettah be a-tryin' on
　　De white probashion gown;
Fus' yo' know all ob a sudden
Mos' yo' coons 'll take to scuddin'
An' dose cushun feet
　　Dey 'll nevah tech de groun'.

PRESQUE ISLE

How well I remember the day that I spent
On that far away island where all is content;
When sweet from the woodland, 'midst bramble and brake,
The birds caroled on—it seemed just for our sake,
Oh, where on this orb is a spot that we feel
The rapture of loving as on the Presque Isle?

I laved in her looks and I bathed in her smiles,
Nor thought of the nook where the serpent beguiles;
I watched the calm glow of her passionate cheek,
As in maidenhood only those blushes can speak.
How I ardently knelt at her feet to reveal
The love that was born far away on Presque Isle.

When the stars had come out in the clear northern skies
They but beamed on my soul, ah! less bright than her eyes,
And I turned in despair from the orbs up above
To gaze in the eyes of an angel of love.

Presque Isle

Our lips met, oh ! why should we longer conceal
Our love on that rapturous, star-lit Presque Isle?

I'm still looking back on that island to-day,
But my lips they are mute—I have nothing to say,
Except that my soul I claim as my own,
Tho' my soft auburn hair is all scatter'd and strown.
And after each cyclone in silence I kneel
And pray for an earthquake to sink the Presque Isle.

BEULAH LAND

OBER de ribber in Beulah Lan'
    De lubly angels in white robes stan';
Dey beckon me dar, I kin hyar de ban',
Ober de ribber in Beulah Lan'.

Ober de ribber what sights I see!
Somebody stan's dar a-waitin' fo me;
Stan's on de sho' ob de Jaspah Sea,
A-callin'; he says dar's res' fo' me.

Ober de ribber I soon mus' go,
Weary ob waitin' fro' all dis woe;
An' when my journey is ended I know
Dat de Good Shepherd will open de do'.

Ober de ribber my soul takes wing,
De songs ob Zion I hyar 'em sing;
When tuned to de harps how our voices will ring
Close 'roun' de frone ob de Hebenly King.

Ober de ribber dey beckon to me,
De ribber dat flows to de Jaspah Sea;

Beulah Land

Ober de ribber you all mus' know
Dat de Good Shepherd will open de do'.

Den we 'll shout glory an' praise 'im an' sing
'Long up de golden streets, how it will ring;
Close to de Massa fo'evah we 'll stan',
Ober de ribber in Beulah Lan'.

THE BLACKBIRD AND THE THRUSH

"IT'S my idee," a blackbird said,
    As he sat in a mulberry bush,
"It's my idee, it seems to me,
    I can warble as well as a thrush."

"Let 'er go, let 'er go," said a carrion crow,
    As he swung on an old clothesline,
"For I won't budge, but I'll act as judge,
    And the winner I'll ask to dine."

In a minor key the thrush sang he,
    'Way up in an elm remote,
And twice and thrice like paradise
    Songs welled from the warbler's throat.

Then a rooster he, in his usual glee,
    Flew up on the barnyard fence,
And he crowed and he crowed; then he said:
      "I'll be blowed
    If that isn't simply immense."

The Blackbird and the Thrush

Then the blackbird, well, he listened a spell
  And began in garrulous run,
But he was n't admired, for a farmer tired—
  Well, he up and fired a gun.

Then the black crow said, as he rested his head:
  "I want to go somewhere and die."
And a young cock-a-too said: "I do, too,"
  And a parrot said: "So do I."

DE SPRING-HOUSE

DOWN to de spring-house am whar I long to wandah—
De ole do' a-creakin' as hit swings to en fro,
Down to de spring-house standin' ovah yondah,
Standin' ovah yondah in de long time ago.

Down by de spring-house de lilacs am a-bloomin';
Hollyhocks a-noddin' an' honeysuckles thick.
Down by de spring-house I listen to de lowin',
An' reckon de ole brindle cow am wadin' up de creek.

Down by de spring-house once again I 'm walkin';
Yellah cream 'pon de shef, kain't let it be.
Down in de spring-house no use in talkin'—
Col' greens an' hog-jole 's good enuff fo' me.

Down to de spring-house missus comes a-callin',
Ol' hound 's a-bahkin an' massa 'gins ter shout.
Down in de spring-house what a caterwaulin'—
Jais sort a-waitin' fo' de niggah to come out.

De Spring-House

Down by de spring-house blackbirds eat de cherry,
Wasp suck de honeysuckle, clovah feed de bee.
Down in de spring-house niggah nevah worry—
Down in de spring-house am good enuff fo' me.

1

UNDER OBLIGATIONS

A NEGRO PARSON'S CHRISTMAS SERMON.

I NOTICE dat de weddah's rathah chilsome, mo' or less,
An' I notice dat de back-log so't o' crackles, Lor' bress ?—
Ole Crimp is on de tuhnpike an' de fross is on de faince
An' Sant' Claus 'll soon be hyah, so chillun, hab saince.

I seed 'im on Ole Massa's ruff; twar jais de oddah night,
Wid a span ob balky reindyahs, bofe um dapple gray an' white.
Dey war hitched to a monsus lookin' alligatah sleigh,
An' filled wid gifts fo' de chillun, piled ebery which un way.

Hab any ob yo' chillun bin a-sinnin' ?
Or a-sassin' yo' suppearyahs, or a-grinnin' ?
Yo' bettah read yo' Bible 'bout ole Moses an' de laws,
Foh yo's undah obligashuns to Ole Santa Claus.

Under Obligations

How many ob yo' chillun bin a-tendin' to de church?
An' done made up yo' minds to leabe de debbil in de lurch,
Hab yo' tended up to Sunday-school, an' listen'd to yo' teachah?
Does yo' always drap a nickel to try an' spote yo' preachah?

Am yo' wilful to yo' faddah or yo' muddah?
Does yuh pestervate yo' sistah or yo' bruddah?
Yo' bettah change yo' tacticks cause, well, jess because
Yo's undah obligashuns now to Ole Santa Claus.

Kin yo' ansuah all dese questions dat yo' pastah has perferd?
Ef yo' kaint, yo' bettah hang yo' haids en neváh say a word;
Foh yo' pastah sort ob reckons dat de debbil's bin bo'n in yuh
An' when ole Santa Claus comes roun' he'll surely be agin yo'.

So, ef any ob yo' chillun bin a-sinnin',
Or a-sassin' yo' suppearyahs, or a-grinnin',
Yo' bettah read yo' Bible, don't yo' hesitate or pause,
Kase yo's undah obligashuns to Ole Santa Claus.

CLEOPATRA AND CHARMIAN

I'M dying, yes, Charmian, dying,
   I'm dying to stroll out awhile.
This eve we'll go down to the Cydnus
   And scare up some old crocodile.

I swear by the Priests of Serapis
   This Egypt just gives me the blues,
It seems that my only companions
   Are crocodiles, storks, and emus.

I'm so melancholy and stupid,
   Sweet maid should I drop in a doze,
I pray you loosen my sandals
   And pull off these long silken hose.

Bring me the asp in the lattice box
   That Tony caught down in the Nile.
Pinch up his tail with a small carob stick
   And then let him wiggle awhile.

Last night my pet lion, Augustus,
   Was howling for something to eat—

Cleopatra and Charmian

Why under the sun do n't they feed him
    That slave with the pigeon-toed feet?

To-day you must polish those idols,
    The buhl-headed idols—and more,
Just see that those lubberly eunuchs
    Do n't spit on my porphry floor.

You 're getting infernally lazy
    And looking so peeked and white.
See here, miss! Does that jay from Memphis
    Think you can sit up every night?

I vow, I believe you 're weak-minded,
    Your brain seems to be in a whirl,
Next week I 'll go down to Miletus
    And look up a new hired girl.

Go bring me my old mother hubbard,
    And also those Indian balms;
Come, let us go down in the gardens
    And bask 'neath those lovely dhoum palms.

Bring also my pearl brooch and necklace,
    Dear, lazy, old Ethiope girl!
Some wine of Ramesian vintage
    I 'll mix up a nectar of pearl.

Cleopatra and Charmian

We'll drink to Osiris and Isis
   The great Sphinx of Theban renown,
Old Cheops, the father of pyramids,
   The Ptolemies, then to the crown.

By Pthah! let us try the new poison
   On some of our new Roman stock.
I'd like to tip over some pyramid
   And give the old mummies a shock.

What's that? Who seeks for admission?
   Was that a fog horn I heard blow?
Can Tony be nearing the castle?
   Just look, Charmian dear, ere you go.

Have something good, dearie, for breakfast,
   But you know what pleases me most—
Some pelican's eggs, a la Cairo,
   And fried phenicopters on toast.

Remember about rising early,
   Get up with the wagtail at four.
So smother the glim in the hallway,
   And lock up the back kitchen door.

BUT THEN

JOHN OSWALD McGUFFIN he wanted to die
  'Nd bring his career to an end ;
Of course, well—he did n't say nothin' to me—
  But that 's what he told every friend.
So one afternoon he went down to the pier,
'Nd folks saw him actin' most terribly queer ;
He prayed 'nd he sung, put his hand up to cough
An' every one thought he was a-goin to jump off—
          But he did n't.
          He may jump tomorrer
          Mornin' at ten—
          Said he was goin' to
          Try it again—
          But then.

John Oswald he said he was tired of the earth—
  Of its turmoil and struggle and strife—
'Nd he made up his mind a long, long time ago
  He was just bound t' take his own life ;
'Nd the very next time 'at he started to shave,

But Then

Determined to die, he wus goin' t' be brave;
So he stood up 'nd flourished the knife in despair
'Nd every one thought 'at he'd kill himself there—
      But he did n't.
      He says 'at tomorrer
      Mornin' at ten
      He has a notion to
      Try it again—
      But then.

He went and bought arsenic, bought paris green,
   'Nd cobalt 'nd all kinds of stuff
'Nd he took great delight in leaving it 'round—
   Of course that was done for a bluff—
Then he rigged up his room with a horrible thing,
That would blow his head off by pullin' a string.
Folks heard the explosion—rushed up—on his bed
John Oswald was lyin'. They whispered, "He's
   dead."
      But he was n't.
      He riz up 'nd said:
      Could n't say when
      He'd fully decide to
      Try it again—
      But then.

PINKEY

I RECKON wintah's goin'
It 's rainin' 'sted of snowin'.
I tale yo' dar 's no knowin'
    Jes' whar dis chile 'll go.

Might go to Souf Kyarlina,
An' summah dar wid Dinah;
I guess I 'd cut a shine
    Among de coons I know.

Den dar 's my good ol' massa
'Way down in Tallahassie.
He ain't fo'got dis sassie
    Chile dat used to sing.

De why he call me "Pinkey"
Was de colluh ob my crinkey
Frock I wore so shrinky
    When I use to dance de fling.

Pinkey

We gals out in de moonshine
Would dance de good ol' coonjine,
An' dreckly den we 'd soon fin'
    Dat missus heah de noise.

Den mighty quick she 'd hurry
Down dar all in a flurry,
An' fin' dis huckleberry
    A-dancin' fo' de boys.

An' den de way she 'd take me,
An' land ob goodness, shake me!
Ol' missus raised an' brake me.
    No wondah I 'se so good.

Ol' missus used to tell me
Dat like de cows she 'd bell me,
Or else she 'd done go sell me
    To Yankees, I 'se so rude.

I 'membah Rasmus Biddle,
As black as auntie's griddle;
He used to play de fiddle,
    An' feet! umh! a holy show.

An' dar was Luke an' Jaspah,
Lucindy, Jude an' Caspah,

Pinkey

Dat ignominyus, 'aspah-
  Ratin', on'ry lookin' moke.

Dat ol' cush-footed, cramp-back,
Dat essence ob ol' lampblack,
Dat inside yih! yih! ob a smokestack,
  Us gals we called 'im smoke.

An' dat new coon f'om Cuba,
Dat use to play de tuba,
He used to pat de juba,
  While I dance de Mobile buck.

De ole banjo was a-pingin'
An' dat pink frock a-swingin',
Dis yaller chile a-wingin',
  Jes' hoein' down fo' luck.

I ain't no Mobile niggah,
I cut no Mobile figgah,
But when yo' pull de triggah
  Yo' pestah dese heah shoes.

An' when de fiddle's scrapin',
Dar 's too much music 'scapin',
I 'se got to git to shapin'
  Myself or git de blues.

Pinkey

Yo' wondah dat I 'se weary
Fro all dese days so dreary,
Dar ain't one fing dat 's cheery
    'Bout Shcawgo life fo' me.

Dat 's de raison dat I 'se goin',
Jes' as soon 'zit quits a-snowin',
An' de col' win' stops a-blowin',
    Back to ole Kyarlina State.

Dar de ivy am a-creepin';
Whar my po' ole muddah 's sleepin';
Missus—'scuse me kase I 'se weepin',
    Seems as if I could n't wait.

THE BUNG TOWN CANAL

DO you remember, Tom, Billy, and Sal,
The old swimmin' days in the Bung Town Canal?
The big millin' logs fast asleep on its banks,
We used to jump off of and cut up odd pranks
In our tropical costume. We used to make Sal
Go home when we swum in the Bung Town Canal.

I never 'll forget it, an' 'tween you an' me,
You 'member the place where the mill uster be?
We had a long spring-board out there 'n we 'd scud
An' jist go head foremost clean inter the mud.
I may fergit some things, but I never shall
Fergit them old times 'round the Bung Town Canal.

Nobody need never say nothin' to me
'Bout the Blue Danube River er banks of the Dee,
They can 't perduce sights like some 'at I 've seen
Crawlin' up on its banks and off in the green
Old marsh where the scum and malarier are,
'S the pizenest things in the world out in there.

The Bung Town Canal

Me an' John Price caught the gol blamedest thing,
With six legs an' four fins 'n a yaller-jack sting,
Two eyes in its head an' two horns in its tail,
An' it carried a shell on its back like a snail,
So we tuck it home an' skeer'd mother an' Sal
'Ith what we fished out of the Bung Town Canal.

Once they's a stranger 'at jest took a drink
From the Bung Town Canal, an' course he didn't think
What he was doin', an' after awhile
He went an' turned yeller, as yeller as bile;
So doctors all went to perscribin' fer him,
Makin' his chances a blamed sight more slim.

What they all said was that he had a snaik
Way down in his stummick an' he better take
One or two whiskeys 'fore eatin' each meal,
Then in a week er two mebbe he'd feel
Better. So natcherly he tuck to drink,
Usin' rye whiskey 'bout three months, I think.

Course havin' snaiks in the stummick is tough,
But snaiks is a-knowin' when they've got enough.
So gittin' dissatisfied, most of 'em fled,
Some hid in his boots and some got in his bed.
I argied the pint 'at he never'd a died
If they'd a jest let 'em be on the inside.

The Bung Town Canal

We buried him there where the low grasses creep,
In a bed of pond-lilies we put him to sleep,
Where the meddy-larks sing and the cry of the loon,
An' the rice-hen is singin' a dolefuller tune.
We left him alone, after writin' his gal
Concernin' his death an' the Bung Town Canal.

Oh, them barefooted days an' the spot where I'd lay
An' jest steeped my hide in the glory o' day,
A-hearin' the bulrushes whisper an' sigh,
An' watchin' the shadder-clouds hurryin' by.
How I long to go back there, with some old-time pal,
'N dive off once agin in the Bung Town Canal.

DE MASSA

DE Massa to de shepa'd say:
Go call de sheep dat's gone astray.
De night is col' I hear de win',
A shakin 'gin my winder blin';
Dars some po' sheep dat's gone astray.
Go call 'em in, Cu-dey! Cu-dey!
    Cu-dey! Cu-dey! Cu-dey!

De shepa'd said de night was col',
But all de sheep was in de fol'.
"I called 'em in at set ob sun;
Dey all come runnin' sep de one
Dat's always wanderin' away,
An' never minds de call Cu-dey!
    Cu-dey! Cu-dey! Cu-dey!"

De massa then went fro' de gloom,
Ob medder fields. De autumn moon
Was dodgin' roun' behin' a cloud,
But still he goes a-callin' loud,
For dat one sheep dat's gone astray.
I hyar him call, "Cu-dey! Cu-dey!
    Cu-dey! Cu-dey! Cu-dey!"

De Massa

He listens long to hyar de soun',
F'om some ole wedder pokin' roun',
Dat's gone to res' down in de dell,
An' wanderin' roun' has los' his bell;
Tho' softer now so far away,
I hyar him call, "Cu-dey! Cu-dey!
   Cu-dey! Cu-dey! Cu-dey!"

But furder on in gloom an' damp,
Upon de border ob de swamp;
So chill'd by dew and autumn win's,
Right dar de po' los' sheep he fin's;
He lifts him up, an leads de way,
Yit I hyar massa's echo say,
"Cu-dey! Cu-dey! Cu-dey! Cu-dey!
   Cu-dey! Cu-dey! Cu-dey!"

An' all night long de win' an' rains,
An' hail against de winder panes,
In dreams I hyar de massa call
De wanderin' sheep, he knows 'em all.
He pints de road, an' shows de way
An' ever stan's an' calls, "Cu-dey!
Cu-dey! Cu-dey! Cu-dey! Cu-dey!
   Cu-dey! Cu-dey! Cu-dey!"

COONIE IN DE HOLLER

COONIE in de holler hidin' hin' de logs,
    Little picaninies ketchin' pollywogs,
Banjo am a ping ping pingin'out a tune,
    Ebery t'ing am lubly as a day in June.

Ping, ping, ping, banjo am a-pingin',
    Sing, sing, sing, yaller gals a-singin',
Wing, wing, wing, ain't dat wingin' fine?
    De same ole step in de ole coonjine.

Cindy in de kitchen tryin' out de lard,
    Jusy in de do'way, rakin' up de yard,
Jaspah am a-pickin' on de ole banjo
    An' he am a-singin' "I'se gwine home to Clo."

Coonie in de holler done gone up a tree,
    An' he am a-hidin' whar no one can see.
But he know his bizness nuff not to come down,
    Kase he know him likely meet dat frocious houn'.

Coonie in de holler, hark, I hyar a gun,
    Git a-goin' Rasmus, Jube git up an' run,

Coonie In De Holler

All de foolish niggahs runnin' till dey pant,
   Bet my bottom dollah Rube has treed an ant.

" Pee, wee, wee," pee wees in de cedars,
   Bluebirds come, robins an' de leaders,
Cudder-rudder-rung, bullfrog just now sung,
   Hyar dat distant thundah; guess dat spring am sprung.

AFTER WEIDENFELLER GOES

IT's goin' to be blamed lonesome after Weidenfeller goes;
Catastrofies are follerin' right and no one knows
What's goin' to happen next, for banks are bustin' every day
An' now we hear the woeful news that Weid's agoin' away.

Weid agoin'! think o' that! not goin' up above,
Nor out upon Midway Plaisance, that spot the boys all love,
Or goin' to Californy or out to Idaho,
But yet they say he's goin' away, that's why we're filled with woe.

O' course he ain't goin' to die or anything like that,
He's simply got his sal'ry raised and kind o' "standin' pat"
With—I believe it's with the boss; I'm bamed if I can tell;
But I know Weid's goin' away—know that mighty well.

After Weidenfeller Goes

I know the Club 'll miss 'im lots; so all the fellers here
Are gathered 'round the festal board to-night to give
    'im cheer.
An' send 'im off in proper shape, which only goes
    to show
We 're mighty glad he 's prosperin' but sad to see
    'im go.

I 've stood upon the wild sea banks, afar in Michigan,
Just left its sandy shores this morn to be here once
    again—
Back here to meet our dear old friend, with heart chock
    full of woe—
An' do n't that show I 'm mournin', too, cause Weid
    has got to go?

God bless 'im, and let fortune smile and cheer 'im
    on each day,
Suckers and fame still tag 'im on an' get right in
    his way,
So if the Club 'pears lonesome when the frosts are
    comin' on,
We 'll sit around an' say it 's jest 'cause Weidenfel-
    ler's gone.

ZACCHEUS

ZACCHEUS clim' up de sycamo' tree,
    A-waitin' fo' de good Lo'd ter come,
Den' 'e looked up de road jes' fur as he could see,
    A-waitin'. fo' de good Lo'd ter come.
Oh, Zaccheus knew he could done see de bes',
Ef 'e clim' up de tree he could ovahlook de press,
An' 'haps 'e could sleep an git a leetle res',
    While a-waitin' fo' de good Lo'd ter come,
Waitin' fo' de good Lo'd ter come elong come,
    A-waitin' fo' de good Lo'd ter come,
        He could ovahlook de press,
        An' 'e git a leetle res'
While a-waitin' fo' de good Lo'd ter come.

Ole Zaccheus set on de bow ob de tree
    Waitin' fo' de good Lo'd ter come,
A long time ago in de ole Judee,
    A-waitin' fo' de good Lo'd ter come.
Along about noontime en ebbery ting clear,
Word went around dat de Lo'd was drawin' near,

Zaccheus

En de press begun to jostle en de multitude to cheer
    While a-waitin' fo' de Lo'd ter come,
Waitin' fo' de good Lo'd to come elong come,
    A-waitin' fo' de good Lo'd ter come.
        When de Lo'd was drawin' near,
        How de folks begun to cheer,
While a-waitin' fo' de good Lo'd ter come.

When de Lo'd come elong 'e said to Zach,
    Waitin' fo' de Lo'd ter come,
"I 'se pow'ful glad yo 's heah, I am, fo' a fac',"
    Waitin' fo' de Lo'd ter come.
"So come right down hyah outen dat tree,
Yo 's jes' de berry pusson I 'se lookin' fo' ter see.
Dis day I abide at de house wid thee,"
    Waitin' fo' de good Lo'd ter come.
Waitin' fo' de Lo'd ter come elong come,
    A-waitin' fo' de good Lo'd ter come,
        De republican an' sinnah,
        Took de Lo'd home to dinnah,
Waitin' fo' de Lo'd ter come.

Now Zaccheus he was an Israelite,
    Waitin' fo' de good Lo'd ter come.
En he lived in a mansion way out o' sight
    While waitin' fo' de Lo'd ter come.

Zaccheus

En Zach knew de Lo'd knew he had stuff
En he wondah'd ef de Lo'd was dun makin' 'im a bluff.
But de Lo'd went home wid Zach shuah enuff,
    A-waitin' fo' de Lo'd ter come.
Waitin' fo' de good Lo'd ter come elong come,
    A-waitin' fo' de good Lo'd ter come—
        Oh, Zaccheus de sinnah,
        Took de good Lo'd to dinnah—
A-waitin' fo' de good Lo'd ter come.

Ole Zaccheus he was a shuah nuff sinnah,
    Waitin' fo' de good Lo'd ter come,
An' back in dem days was a seven time winner,
    A-waitin' fo' de Lo'd ter come.
But de Lo'd told Zach he mus' gib to de po'
En neber let a beggah man pass his do'.
Den Zach he said: "I will Lo'd, sho',"
    While a-waitin' fo' de good Lo'd ter come.
Waitin' fo' de good Lord ter come elong come.
    A-waitin' fo' de good Lo'd ter come.
        So gib me de po'
        Dat pass by yo' do',
While a-waitin' fo' de good Lo'd ter come.

A RETROSPECTION

I 'SE a sittin' neaf de ole magnolia tree
So't o' thinkin' ob de times dat used to be,
In de huckleberry patches
When we heah'd the steamah Natchez,
An' de white folks all u'd hustle down to see.
Dar was Missy Elenor an' Julie Ann,
An' Haidee Lee, who lived wid Uncle Dan.
    But she went and run'd away,
    An' de folks set up an' say
Dat she 'loped off wid a wicked no'then man.

Po' Cindy she is daid, and Aunty Mary
Doan do nuffin' now but sate aroun' en worry;
    En ebery night she say
    She 'specks to go next day,
But her disease ain' one dat 'pears to hurry.
De doctors seems es ef dey had n't made out
What 't is das makes ole aunty look so played out;
    But de time she will consume
    Turnin' Heaven into gloom
Will make de Lo'd repent when sh 's done laid out.

A Retrospection

Missie Elenor she married Col. Paxton,
An' de scandal 'bout the colonel 'do n't be axin',
    But dey say, I undahstan',
    Dat he done shot off his han',
Jes' to keep from jinin' good ole Stonewall Jackson.
An' Julie Ann dat talk like she was hoarse,
Dat huzzy she 's done gone an' got divorce.
    Dey lived in Chicamauga
    Till she moved up to Chicagah,
Kase tings is mighty cheap up dar ob course,

Yo' 'membah Haidee Lee? I undahstan'
Dat she 's trablin' roun' de country wid a band,
    An' heah she sort o' prances
    Wid a skirt an' thinks she dances,
Did you evah, evah, goodness land!
Wid de 'vantages dey used to hab en' see
How dem girls was all turned out. Now can it be
    Dat cussidness is sown,
    Or is it in de bone?
Well, hit mus' be in de family, seems to me.

ST. PATRICK'S DAY

MAVOURNEEN, swate Isle,
    I am lonely widout thee,
I sigh for your hills an' your calm sky so blue;
    Shure I niver had cause
    One shmall moment to doubt thee,
An' whin I 'm not thinkin' I 'm dhreamin' of you.

Chorus.

    So lads, whin I call ye's,
    Come sing your "Come all Ye's,"
Ah! here 's to ould Ireland, byes, ivery toime:
    Och, coleens, be aisy,
    Your dhrivin' me crazy,
What day of our counthry is one half so foine?

    St. Patrick's the day, shure,
    It was in the mornin',
An' oh! how it graved me, Mavourneen, to part;
    But I left ye's, as I
    Left me mother, a-mournin'
An' kissin' the shamrock she placed near me heart.

St. Patrick's Day

    I'm sorry I left ye's
    To cross the deep wather,
For the game that I've played wid misfortune's a
    draw;
    But do n't ye be ailin',
    I'll soon be a-sailin'
Away to the Isle of swate "Erin go Bragh."

    Then lend me the harp
    And I'll wake "Tipperary,"
Sing "By Killarney" wid "Noreen Maureen";
    The shamrock I'm pressin',
    An' while I'm confessin'
I'm praisin' St. Patrick an' "wearin' the green."

INJUN SUMMAH

D^E Injun summah's comin',
De bees is all froo hummin',
De watah-mellon thumbin'
  Has passed long time ago.
De ole clock in de kitchen
Is tickin' mos' bewitchin',
While Gabe is out unhitchin'
  Just kase it looks like snow.

De lambs is runnin' over
De aftahmath ob clovah,
An' yondah comes de drovah;
  I 'spec he ' got a yahn
About de ole bell-weddah
Dat 's wand'rin roun' de meddah
An' wants ter git togeddah
  Wid de sheep up roun' de bahn.

Some days de sun is shinin',
Some days de win' is whinin',

Injun Summah

An' den I'se after fin'in'
  Big pippins on de groun';
De birds hab all stopped singin',
Wil' geese is soufward wingin',
Jes' look an' see 'em stringin'
  Whar warmah weddah's foun'.

De yaller cat is nappin'
En layin' roun' an' gappin';
Bimeby he will be slappin'
  Some tom-cat on de wall.
Dar's a mellah, yellah glory
Kase de yeah is ol' an' ho'ry,
An' a melancholy story
  So't o' hangin' roun' us all.

'CAUSE IT'S GITTIN' SPRING

THE medder lark is pipin' forth a sweeter note to me,
And I hear the pewees over yonder in the cedar tree ;
The popple leaves is quiv'rin' 'cause the wind is in the west,
And the robin's 'round a-hookin' straws to build hisself a nes' ;
The blackbird he 's a-flashin' up the crimson on his wing.
    What 's the reason ?
    Oh, the reason's 'cause it 's gittin' spring.

The old man's got the rheumatiz an' stiff as he can be ;
Why it do n't git settled weather's moah'n he can see ?
But when it clears off splendid, then he 's feared the crops is lost,
An' he reckons jest a little wind 'ud keep away the frost.
The kitchen door is open ; I can hear Elmiry sing.
    What 's the reason ?
    Oh, the reason's 'cause it 's gittin' spring.

'Cause It's Gittin' Spring

The air is kind o' soft'nin' and you think it's goin' to storm;
Sometimes it's kind o' chilly, then again it comes off warm;
An' jest when it's the stillest you can hear the bull-frog's note,
An' it 'pears as if he wonder'd how the frost got in his throat.
The ducks and geese are riotous, an' strainin' hard to sing.
          What's the reason?
Oh, the reason's cause it's gittin' spring.

DECORATE DE CABIN

I 'SE done gwine ter decorate mah cabin,
Wid all de brick-er-brack I 'se been a-habbin',
    Den I 'se boun' ter hunt er wife,
    'Deed I is, yo' bet yo' life.
Dar 's nuffin like a woman roun' er blabbin'.

I 'se gwine ter hang a coon skin on de do',
En hab some Turkey rugs roun' on de flo';
    An' I nevah yet hab seen
    De ole cabin look ser clean,
Ef yo' peep in dar some time yo 'll fin' it so.

I los' mah wife las' summah, Jane Safras,
Kase she done got up 'n blew out de gas,
    An' eber since her leabin'
    I 'se been a sort o' greebin,
But I hope de one I 'se ketchin' now 'll las'.

We 's gwine ter start right in to decoratin',
An' yo' 'll be surprised at what I 'm statin',

Decorate De Cabin

    She 's six feet high en taperin',
    En out ob sight in paperin',
I 'se mighty glad I 'se been so long a-waitin'.

We 's gwine ter 'range de pictures on de wall—
Yo' talk about a fine reception hall—
    Yo' ought to see de flowahs,
    En de chromios in ours,
W'y, de white man's house ain' in de thing at all.

THE ULTIMATUM

"YOU can decorate your office
    With a thousand gilded signs,
And have upholstered furniture
    In quaint antique designs;
Have the latest patent telephone
    Where you can yell 'Hello!'
But," said she, "I just made up my mind
    That typewriter must go.

"You can stay down at the office,
    As you have done, after hours;
And, if you are partial to bouquets,
    I'll furnish you with flowers.
You can spring the old club story
    When you come home late, you know,
But, remember, I've made up my mind
    That typewriter must go.

"You can let your bookkeepers lay off
    And see a game of ball;

The Ultimatum

The office-boy can leave at noon
    Or not show up at all.
There—what is this upon your coat?
    It is n't mine I know.
I think I know a thing or two—
    That typewriter shall go."

DREAMY DAYS

OH! the dreamy days of youth,
In appearance how uncouth,
As we waded through the frog ponds and
    The ditches.
With big patches on each knee,
And where they had n't ought to be.
Oh! the days when one suspender
    Held our breeches.

Oh! the dreamy days of yore,
And the slippery cellar door.
Oh! that cherry tree whose fruit we oft
    Were testing.
Then we'd wait till after tea,
When we'd sing with doleful glee.
Oh! how often mother made it
    Interesting.

WHEN THE STAGE GITS IN

PAP 'LL git a letter, 'nd Uncle Zed a book,
'Nd Aunty Jane expects er magazine;
   'Nd school 'll all be out,
   'Nd the children run 'nd shout,
While a-playin' "one-old-cat" out on the green.
   An' the men 'at's in the grocery store
   'Ll come outside 'nd stand
'Nd talk, 'nd look around 'nd grin;
   Fer the folks down at the post-office
   A-standin' all around
Are happy when the stage gits in.

Ma has done the bakin', 'nd made some patty cakes,
'Nd Lizzie has done the sweepin' all alone;
   An' she's dustin' up the furniture
   'Nd settin' things about,
'Cause tomorry we're expectin' Aunt Se'phrone.
   Nan has had 'er hair did up
   In papers all night long,

When The Stage Gits In

'Nd to-day she's a-frizzin' it agin;
I bet you any money she's expectin' some one, too,
'At 'll be here when the stage gits in.

When you see the yaller cat begin a-washin' up,
An' 'er hind leg pinted over that way, some
      Folkses allers say it is
      The surest kind o' sign
'At company is liable to come.
'Nd when the parlor's opened a sort o' funny smell
Comes 'cause the fire's kindled up ag'in;
      We're goin' to have a high old time
      'Nd all our relatives
'Ill be here when the stage gits in.

THE CULTURED GIRL AGAIN

SHE was so esthetic and culchud,
    Just doted on Wagner and Gluck;
And claimed that perfection existed
    In some foreign English bred duke.

She raved over Browning and Huxley,
    And Tyndal, and Darwin, and Taine;
And talked about flora and fauna,
    And many things I can't explain.

Of Madame Blavatski, the occult,
    Theosophy, art, and then she
Spoke of the Cunead Sibyl
    And Venus de Med-i-che.

She spoke of the why and the wherefore,
    But longed for the whither and whence;
And she said yclept, yip, yap and yonder
    Were used in alliterative sense.

Well, I like a fool sat dumfounded,
    And wondered what she did n't know.

The Cultured Girl Again

'T was 10 when I bade her good evening,
    I thought it in season to go.

I passed her house yesterday evening,
    I do n't know, but it seems to me,
She was chasing around in the kitchen,
    And getting things ready for tea.

I heard her sweet voice calling: "Mother,"
    It was then that I felt quite abashed,
For she yelled, "How shall I fix the 'taters,
    Fried, lionized, baked, biled, or mashed?"

DE CUSHVILLE HOP

I 'SE gwine down to de Cushville hop
   An' dar ain' no niggahs gwine ter make me stop;
Missus gwine to deck me all up in white,
So watch de step dat I 'se gettin' in ter night.
Um-hm, my honey, tain' no use;
Um-hm, my honey, turn me loose,
Um-hm, my honey, watch me shine
When mah foot am a-shakin' in de ole coonjine.

No black niggahs come foolin' roun' me,
I 'se jes' to look at, anyone can see;
I 'se jes' a orniment, an' I mus' 'fess
No niggah put 'is ahm roun' mah snow-white dress
Um-hm, niggah, keep away, understand?
Um-hm, niggah, look out fo' yo' hand;
I 'se jes' ter gaze at I must 'fess,
So do n't put yo' ahm roun' mah snow-white dress.

Bring out de banjo, plunk-plank-pling,
Watch de motion of mah step 'an mah swing;

De Cushville Hop

Do n't yo' pestah me or make me stop
When I git in motion at de Cushville hop.
Um-hm, niggah, keep away, keep away !
Um-hm, niggah, not ter day !
Keep away from me kase I done kain't stop :
I 'se jes' caught mah motion fo' de Cushville hop.

GORD ONLY KNOWS

I SAW an old beggar dis mawnin', Lucindy,
De weathaw was col' an' bleak an' windy,
    An' de fros' took hold
    Ob de end ob his nose.
    Whar wus he goin'?
    Gord only knows, chile,
    Gord only knows.

All he had on was an ole woolen jacket.
An' pants dat had done seed a mighty ha'd racket,
    His shoes war all out,
    Kase I saw his toes.
    Whar wus he goin'?
    Gord only knows, chile,
    Gord only knows.

He said his gran'chillun had turned him away,
Wid nuffin' to eat on las' Thanksgibin' Day.
    Wid no ovahcoat,
    He looked about froze.
    Whar was he goin'?
    Gord only knows, chile,
    Gord only knows.

Gord Only Knows

He lifted his han's, day was bony an' blue,
An' axed me was dis hyar de main avenue,
    Den walked ovah dar
    To dose ten'ment rows.
    Had he friends in dar?
    Gord only knows, chile,
    Gord only knows.

I doan bleb in treatin' a gran'fader so,
Kase some day it's comin' right squar back yer know.
    An' when we grow ole
    An' come to de snows,
    Den who'll keer fo' us?
    Gord only knows, chile,
    Gord only knows.

Gord keeps account ob de sparrers dat fall,
We stan' a-waitin' we soon hyar him call.
    Gord brings de wintah,
    De rain an' de snows,
    Gord makes de win' blow,
    But jes' whar it goes,
    Gord only knows, chile,
    Gord only knows.

JES' TAKE MY ADVICE

JES' a little sunshine, jes' a little rain,
Jes' a little happiness, jes a little pain.
Jes' a little verselet sounds mighty nice
'Bout some oddah business; jes' take my advice.

Jes' a little chicken-coop standin' neah de fence;
Jes' a little dahkey, too, widout a bit ob sense;
Jes' a little pressin' by de fahmer on de triggah,
Jes' a little 'splosion, den a perforated niggah.

Jes' a little lazy coon 'roun' a-shootin' craps,
Den a-buyin' policies 'roun' de lottery traps;
Jes' a little out ob cash, jes' a little stuck;
Jes' a little hungry, jes' a niggah's luck.

Jes' a little bettin' on de faverite in de race;
Jes' a little ways behin', workin' hard fo' place;
Jes' a little money won by dat oddah moke.
Jes' a little ting like dat lef' dis dahkey broke.

Jes' a little pressin' on de latch, wid no one in;
Jes' a little jewelry, jes' a diamond pin;
Jes' a little sheriff on a niggah's trail.
Jes' sech little tings as dat got dis coon in jail.

PATRIOTISM AND A PENSION

OLE Fo'th ob July
  Am mighty close by,
Kase I dnoe smell powdah in de ahr;
  An' de beatin' ob de drums
  When de regiment comes
Sort o' 'minds me ob de times in de wah.

  I was chief ob a division
  Dat furnished de pervision,
An' I done looked wid pride on mah troops;
  I haid em so well drilled
  Dat none ob dem got killed—
Ouah bizness was inspectin' chicken coops.

  I was shot froo de lip,
  An' wounded in de hip,
En fractuah'd mo' er less about de haid;
  At de trouble 'roun' Fo't Pickens
  I was skirmagin' fo' chickens,
When mah foot slipt an' I fell off de shaid.

Patriotism and a Pension

    Gen'l Sherman gib us right
    To forage mos' de night,
So dat's why I 'se trompin' on dis paig.
    I was out abductin' salt,
    When somebody hollahed "halt!"
An' de fool up an' shot me in de laig.

    Jais what I want ter mension
    Is, I want increase ob pension,
An' I make mah affidavit fo' de judge
    Dat I was in comman'
    When a shell bust in mah hand,
An' fo' fohty-seben days I could n't budge.

    I'll stop, en hol' mah peace,
    Ef I get a good increase;
I want mah pension bill increased to five;
    Foh mah lip, en hip, an' hand,
    En mah haid, yo' unde'stan',
An' one jes' fo' comin' out alive.

THE OLD MUSICIAN'S FATE

HE played so many instruments
    A thousand won't express
The number that he handled—why
    'T was mor 'n that, I guess;
An' when he got to playin' hard
    We could n't make 'im stop;
It seemed he did n't want to rest
    Er ever take a drop.
He 'd look around fer things to play,
    Then walk up to the viol
As if he 'd suddenly forgot,
    An' touch up that awhile.
The mandolin was his best holt—
    He jest took the diploma
With his Philomela, Tierra
    Del Fuego, La Paloma.
He played an upright pianner forté,
    A concert grand, or square,
And he imitated Paddy
    Roofski, all accept the hair.

The Old Musician's Fate

You should have heard him when he played
    Upon an old trombone
That song about the moments when
    One wants to be alone.
He played upon an Æolian,
    Told us how he used to roam
An' play "Little Sally Waters"
    Ten thousand miles from home.
He played a big church organ great,
    Played with his hands and feet,
And often played the choir, too.
    Oh, it was just a treat.
He played the jewsharp, hit the pipe,
    And worked the organette;
He played not only instruments,
    But everyone he met.
He played 'em all; you should have heard
    Him jerk a grewsome tune
And play those eozoic notes
    Upon a long bassoon.
He played the soft guitar an' scraped
    The tuneful violin;
Old "number five" was his best holt.
    He used to sit and grin,
An' jest ketch up the instruments

The Old Musician's Fate

One right after another ;
It did n't make no difference,
  For one was good as t'other.
Strange instruments—the lyre and lute
  And others that he tooted.
You took your choice. He did n't care
  Whether he fifed or fluted.
He'd rather play 'an anything,
  Unless it was to drink,
Because he said it rested 'im
  An' gave 'im time to think.
He made some curious instruments
  That nobody could play,
And said 'at he would jest about
  Surprise us all some day.
And so one time he fetched 'er out,—
  Of all the lookin' things,
With harps an' horns attached to 'er
  An' run criss-cross with strings.
He brought 'er forth an' sat 'er down
  As if he knew his biz,
And when we asked him what it was?
  He answered, "What it is."
We laughed as we were seated 'round ;
  I recollect 'twas June ;

The Old Musician's Fate

It rained that spring, rained all this morn,
    And rained that afternoon.
There seemed a touch of magic in
    The deftness of his hand;
A look about his pallid face
    We did n't understand.
The instrument we noted much,
    It had such curious stringin',
The frets arranged in such a way;
    He'd made it so for singin',
Then touching on a happy theme
    That carried us remote,
To sunset lands, for melody
    Divine was in each note.
We listened to the lullabies
    Till all were silent, stilled,
In memory of the bygone days,
    The eyes of all were filled.
Then on to sterner manhood and
    Old age. Ah! how he played!
We saw again life's pathway, too;
    But oh! how far we'd strayed.
Then on to sunken cheeks we pass,
    From life then on to glory.

The Old Musician's Fate

O song ! O dirge ! O sainted theme !
   Sad requiem to life's story.

That pallid look now comes again,
   The tremors o'er him creep.
His head falls back. Dead ? No, my friend,
   He's simply gone to sleep.

THE PESSIMIST*

NOTHING to do but work,
    Nothing to eat but food,
Nothing to wear but clothes
    To keep one from going nude.

Nothing to breathe but air
    Quick as a flash 't is gone;
Nowhere to fall but off,
    Nowhere to stand but on.

Nothing to comb but hair,
    Nowhere to sleep but in bed,
Nothing to weep but tears,
    Nothing to bury but dead.

Nothing to sing but songs,
    Ah, well, alas! alack!
Nowhere to go but out,
    Nowhere to come but back.

*Sometimes published under the title "The Sum of Life."—PUBS.

The Pessimist

Nothing to see but sights,
    Nothing to quench but thirst,
Nothing to have but what we've got;
    Thus thro' life we are cursed.

Nothing to strike but a gait;
    Everything moves that goes.
Nothing at all but common sense
    Can ever withstand these woes.

A RECORD F'OM WAY 'BACK

    Y O' spose I 'se gwine ter cuh-comb
       An' boddah wid dis nag
Ef I low'd he was n't evah gwinter go?
    Why chile, yo' make me tiahed!
    Dis ve'y hoss was siahed
By Pokehontas fohty yeahs ago.

    I 'se doctahed up his wheezin',
    An' done stopped him ob his sneezin';
En pahsley cuahed de spavin on his baik;
    Ef he was n't quite so bulky,
    I'd put him 'foah de sulky,
An' lait yo' see his motion on de traik.

    'Ceptin' froo de wintah, las' yeah
    I haid him out to pastuah;
But de famah said he did n't hab no saince.
    Dar's nuffin 'll keep 'im quiet
    When he gits down on 'is diet,
An' once 'e eat a whole bahb-wiah faince.

A Record F'om Way 'Back

De way I come to buy 'im
Was, de day I come to try 'im
I 'se dumb-foundered wid de way he tuk de bit,
    An' as I was on mah way baik,
    He kerlided wid a hay stack,
An' hi could n't coax 'is tenshun offen hit.

    Yo' notice dat he winks, sah,
    He 's comin' out de kinks, sah ;
An' mine yo' doan go nyah his heels at all,
    Kase 'e's nuhvas an' 'e's dangus,
    An' speshly so to strangus,
An' hi nevah 'low no pusson 'roun' 'is stall.

    He 's pow'ful fond ob grazin'
    An' his appytite's amazin' ;
Dat 's a sho sign dat 'e's got good bottom to 'im.
    When I bought 'im 'e's so thin
    Dat 'e could n't ketch 's win',
An' Rasmus, yo' could read a papah thro' 'im.

    I tale yo' he 's a hummah,
    'Low I 'll show de folks dis summah,
Kase jes' now he aint feelin' zackly bright,
    When he gets 'is second win' sah,
    Yo' ought to see him spin, sah,
Why, chile, dat hoss's reckod 's out ob sight.

THANKSGIBBIN IN OLE VIRGINNY

TER-DAY'S Thanksgibbin',
    En good lan' er libbin',
Go gib de old hoss er double mess o' co'n.
    Ole pot bubble
    Possum's in trouble,
An' we's gwine ter feas' upon 'im sho 's yo' bo'n.
Nigger wid de long straw he git de possum;
  Nigger wid de nex' straw de jack rabbit; den
Nigger wid de nex' one he gets de turkey,
  But de short straw done draw de little Guinea hen.
    De little speckle' hen,
    De little Guinea hen,
Little pickaninny has ter eat de Guinea hen.

    Ter-day 's Thanksgibbin',
    Good lan' er libbin'.
Po' ole beggah-man comes knockin' at de do';
    Gib 'im off yo' table
    Long as yo' is able,

Thanksgibbin In Ole Virginny

Kase poverty an' hunger may sometime come to yo'.
Darky wid de long straw he git de possum,
   Darky wid de nex' straw de jack rabbit; den
Darky wid de nex' one he git de turkey,
   But de short straw done draw de litttle Guinea hen.
        De little speckle' hen,
        De little Guinea hen,
De short straw done draw de little Guinea hen.

GRAVE MATTERS

W'EN dis ole man comes ter die,
    Death is mos' unsightly;
Doan' yo' lay me in no room
Wid de pull-down curtain gloom;
'Taint de place de dead should stay
W'en de spirit's gone away,
    Off ter where hit 's brightly.

'Struct de pa'son 'fore he 'gins,
    Tetch the subject tritely;
Kase hit 's gen'ly undahstood
I hain't been so pow'ful good;
An' fo' him ter shout an' groan
'Bout me settin' roun' de frone,
    'Low hit won't look rightly,

W'en de fun'al 'gins ter start,
    Shove mah box in tightly.
'Membah I is in de hearse;
Yo' am comin', but I 'se firs'.

Grave Matters

Ef de mo'ners grieve and mope,
So 's ter make de hosses lope,
    Keep de team up sprightly.

Lowah me slowly in de grave;
    Drap de earf down lightly.
Need n't linger long, and, say,
'Spense wid prayer 's de better way;
Do n't keer ef nobody sings.
Jes' ter know de chu'ch bell rings
    'S gwine ter please me might'ly.

COMIN' CHRISTMAS MORN

I 'M goin' to start next Saturday;
    It won't take more 'n a day
To visit the United States
    In my new toboggan sleigh.
I've sent Jack Frost ahead o' me
    To sort o' find a road,
So my deers 'll find it easy
    'Cause I've got an awful load.

But they've had lots o' exercise,
    An' know the way by sight;
I've speeded them to Baffin's Bay
    An' back here 'fore 't was night.
An' once I drove to Puget's Sound
    An' once to Behring Sea;
I had ter make a trip up there
    To get a Christmas tree.

I wish 't you all could see my house,
    Built out o' cakes 'o ice;

Comin' Christmas Morn

I guess you think it cold inside,
    But no, it's awful nice.
All carpeted with sealskin rugs,
    An' ermine, mink and sable;
I'm going to keep it furnished so
    As long as I am able.

An' no gomphobers in the north
    Can steal 'round unawares,
Because my castle's guarded by
    Two great big polar bears.
So if a burglar man should come
    An' try to break into it
They 'ud squeeze his life out in a jif,
    I've taught 'em how to do it.

Just right around behind my house
    Is where I keep the toys,
'At I am comin' south'ard with,
    Fer all good girls an' boys.
My big cold storage warehouse stands
    Right by a frozen tarn,
An' right along aside o' it
    I have my reindeer's barn.

So never mind, they're both piled full
    Of everything on earth,

Comin' Christmas Morn

With Christmas gifts till you can't rest,
    I do n't know what they 're worth.
An' four big sea dogs set outside
    Two walruses, a seal
That knows so much if you 'd come nigh
    He 'd be the first to squeal.

The purtiest sight you ever saw,
    'S when things is lit up nights—
You know we do n't have gas up here,
    But use the Northern Lights.
An' forth from every icicle
    A dazzle spreads away
That turns the hull big frozen zone
    Into one mighty day.

From where I live I 'd have you know,
    It 's truth upon my soul,
I do n't have very far to go
    To see the big North Pole,
Where Uncle Sam has pinned his flag,
    There 's where the cold wind pipes,
And flaunts the emblem of the brave,
    The proud old stars and stripes.

I 'm coming, children, coming, yes,
    You ought to see my sleigh,

Comin' Christmas Morn

And hear the tinkle, tinkle, as
    I speed along the way,
Through forests bare, o'er snowy plains.
    As sure as you are born,
Old Santa Claus is coming, and
    Will be here Christmas morn.

SAD FATE OF YIM YOHNSEN

AY been har een deese country
    Fem yar go laist week;
Ay been smart Norwehians—
    Ay keets on pooty quvick.

Ven Ay kem har Ay see beg krode
    Of fallers, en Ay tal
Ay vants mae go pooty bad
    To da Stockholm hotal.

De bus mans say vere you kem fram?
    Ay say by Kopenhagen.
Hae puss mae rate troo krode
    An' get mae in his vagen.

Next day get yob in engine-hus;
    Dae fomans he like mae.
Hae rase mae vadgses leeta vile;
    Ay tank Ay stay vade hae.

Ay get mae quainted nice gal,
    Her nam is Christina Yohnsen;

Sad Fate of Yim Yohnsen

She been har bote hawixteen yar,
    She kem hare bay Visconsen.

She say she verk Saidgeveck street
    By da Norway hotel;
She got blue eye en some rade hair—
    Ay laka hare pooty val.

Ay ask hare dake a street-car rade,
    She say she tank she voke;
Ay voke by hare to Lincoln Park
    En have a pooty good talk.

She call mae hare partickley frande
    En den I tank she say,
"Who vill be my papie
    Ven Yim is gone avay?"

Pooty quvick she see vooman frande
    En den she say to mae:
"Mister Yohnsen, please excoose mae,
    Ay vill meed yo' after tea."

En leeta vile Ay tank Ay go
    To da Stockholm hotel.
Ay meese mae money, vatch en chain;
    Ay feel mae not real vell.

Sad Fate of Yim Yohnsen

Ay drink mae alcoholen,
    Bote fifteen glass, en svair;
Ay fight mae two policemans
    Ay tank Ay soon gets squair.

Dae call patrolen vagen
    En Ay rade to da yail;
Ay stay mae dare 'bout fem day,
    Den Ay kem out on bail.

Ay tell da yustice man abote
    De rade-head gal Ay seen;
Da krode of fallers laugh en say
    Dat ya is pooty green.

Chicago konty vare bad place,
    Ay loose mae vadgses all;
Ay take mae trunk to depot train
    En go mae by Santa Pol.

LEGEND OF THE ST. JOSEPH

THERE'S a place, 'pon my soul,
Called the "Old Devil's Hole,"
By the Chippewa chief, Black Otter,
Who, when business was damp,
Went into his camp,
And filled up with fierce fire water.

Then over the river
Over the river
He called to his squaw, Maumee,
"Go get my canoe,
And you may come too,
And bring little Walle-wo-ge."

So off to the river
They all flew the ground,
"Black Otter" as brave as could be,
And the little pappoose—
He could n't get loose—
Was strapped to the back of Maumee.

Legend of the St. Joseph

They floated till dark,
When the wolf's weird bark
Frightened the wits of Maumee;
So she loosened the sack,
Tied fast to her back,
That contained little Walle-wo-ge.

"Black Otter" bent low
And reached for his bow,
When the boat tipped up on its side,
And in fell he, with his squaw Maumee;
And the boat set free, with Walle-wo-ge,
Sped swiftly along with the tide.

Down the swift river's tide
The pappoose took a ride;
The canoe shot along like a rocket,
But he lay there as snug
As a bug in a rug,
Or an old woolen glove in a pocket.

On, on, out to sea
Drifted Walle-wo-ge,
With his face pointed up to the skies;
And history says,
Which is true, more or less,
That the gray sea gulls pecked out his eyes.

Legend of the St. Joseph

Black Otter was drowned
And never was found;
But they say that old Squaw Maumee
Waded back thro' the damp
Of the marsh to the camp
In search of her Walle-wo-ge.

Came back thro' the swale,
And the rain and the hail,
By the side of the waters so blue,
In search of her baby,
To pick him up, may be,
I wish this would all come out true.

Her spirit distressed,
She beat on her breast,
For the poor old squaw's grief knew no bound;
But Monets so swift,
Bore her off in a skiff,
To the land of the famed hunting ground.

On the ninth of November,
I hope you'll remember,
A phantom one plainly can see
Walk down from the hole,
In search of the soul
Of poor little Walle-wo-ge.

Legend of the St. Joseph

Now, this is the legend
Of this old-time region,
And the tale of the Squaw Maumee,
Likewise old Black Otter,
Who fell in the water,
And poor little Walle-wo-ge.

LITTLE JUDE

PO' little Jude, why, doan' yo' know
Dat little chile ? A yeah ago
Her muddah died. I reckon now
'Twais jais las' spring I' se tellin' yo'
    'Bout little Jude.

Po' little waif indeed she war ;
An' how she cried, jes' out de crib
Dat baby war an' her muddah died.
Could walk an' run an' jabbah some,
Dat little Jude. Hit make me cry,
Tale yo' hit do, jes' when I tink
    'Bout little Jude.

De fun'al day she war asleep,
Tuckt in de crib, dat little chile
Had on her bib—dat orfin Jude.
De mo'ners come ; an' when dey pray
Dat little Jude waked up an' say :
" Mammie ! Mammie ! " jes' dat way.
Nobody know jes' what to do
    Wid little Jude.

Little Jude

She cry so ha'd dey lif' her down;
F'om room to room she toddled roun'
A-cryin': "Mammie! come an' take
Yo' little Judy dat's awake—
Yo' little Judy's wide awake."
My lan'! de teahs come in my eyes!
But when she foun' her own high chaih,
Dat had been hid an' pushed it up
'Long side ob whah her muddah was,
An' den climbed up an' pounded on
De coffin-lid, I could n't stan'
De awful grief—de sobs an' teahs—
An' little Jude, a-lookin' roun'
Foh one dat now at las' she's foun'—
While, chile I kai n't—I nevah will
     Fo'get dat day.

LITTLE PUCKEN SINGER

AE tank Ae gal bae "ote a sate,"
    She bae Little Pucken singen.
Har eyes bae bright, lake stars bae nate,
    An bae gol, mae ears bae ringen
        Vare much,
Ven Ae lave dae teeter hus.

Des var fane gal bae drass in vate—
    She bae des contraldo singen.
Ae tank sometime sha bae yust lak
    Dere fairies tengs, vid clingen
        Drasses on,
Ven Ae lave dae teeter hus.

Des songs sha sings bae "Do Ce Las,"
    Bae des Spanish langvage written
Dae pootiest teng, Ae tank, der vas
    En al des vorld. Ae tank Ae smitten
        Ved har
Ven Ae lave dae teeter hus.

Little Pucken Singer

Ae go an see har avry nate,
    (Ae vonder vot sha tanks bae mae?)
An sit al time bae dae front sate,
    An look bae har. Ae tank Ae bae
        Beg fools,
Ven Ae lave dae teeter hus.

But al de same Ae go vonce more,
    Yust for von glance bae har pooty eyes,
Dae make mae heart stop. Den Ae fale sore
    Vare much. Ae tank ets al lies—
        Dose eyes,
Ven Ae lave dae teeter hus.

Ae tank des gale bae "ote a sate:"
    She bae Little Pucken singen,
Har eyes bae bright, like stars bae nate,
    An bae gol, mae ears bae ringen
        Vare much,
Ven Ae lave dae teeter hus.

DOWN IN WALHALLALAH

I PUT flowers on Leeda's grave
    Down in Walhallalah ;
Flowers that in the spring she gave,
Asking me to cherish, save,
Still I placed them on her grave
    Down in Walhallalah.

Tender rains came down at night,
    Down in Walhallalah,
Took the flowers I had pressed
Tenderly to earth and blessed ;
They returned, ah ! newly dressed,
    Down in Walhallalah.

But one flower I had pressed
    Down in Walhallalah,
Did not find its way up through
With the violets so blue
And the marigolds that grew
    Down in Walhallalah.

Down in Walhallalah

Ah ! farewell for evermore ;
    Farewell, Walhallalah,
Tender rains from ashen skies
Never more can ope the eyes
Of the angelhood that lies
    Cold in Walhallalah.

Withered hopes, how like my soul,
    Down in Walhallalah,
Never more shall rise and bloom ;
Such the fate of love.   The doom
Of all is but the tombed gloom
    Down in Walhallalah.

SANTA'S PRESENTS FO' DE GOOD

L ISTEN, chil'un, en I 'll tale yo'
What I seed de odder night
When de snow had so't o' cover'd
    All de house top up in white.
'Way off yonder in de distance
    'Pear'd es ef I seed a road,
En I heard de raindeers rassle
    Wid de bigges' kind o' load.
Den I heard ole Santie whistle,
    En I low I heard 'im sing,
But I know I heard 'is sleigh bells
    Wid a so't o' 'culiah ring.
Den 'e stopt 'is sled a minute
    En I listen'd well 's I could,
En 'e sang : " I 'm on mah journey,
    But hit 's only fo' de good."

Santa's Presents fo' de Good

Den jingle, jingle, jingle,
    I could heah de sleigh bells ring,
Hit was jingle, jingle, jingle,
    Den I heard ole Santie sing:
"I am on mah Chris'mus journey,
    En I 'spose hit's undahstood
Dat I only 'stribute presents
    Whar de chil'un mighty good.

"I ride ovah de house-tops
    En I listen to de noise,
Ef I hear de leastes' trouble dere
    Twix little girls en boys,
Ef I heah 'em quarrelin', cryin',
    Er see 'em wear a frown,
I jes take out my mem'rand
    En chalk dere number down.
Den I so't o' tech mah reindeers
    En I ride ter ebery house,
En I linger neah de chimblys
    Whar hit's quiet as a mouse,
Kase I like it whar hit's peaceful.
    W'en I heah 'em go upstairs
En kneel down by de trundle bed
    En say dere ebenin' pray'rs,

Santa's Presents fo' de Good

Den I listen, listen, listen,
    Kase yo' see hit 's undahstood
Dat I 'm leabin' presents mos'ly
    Whar de chil'un mighty good.

Hit was jingle, jingle, jingle,
    I could heah de sleigh bells ring,
Hit was jingle, jingle, jingle,
    Jes' jingle, jingle, jing.
"I am on mah Chris'mus journey,
    En I 'low hit 's undahstood
Dat I 'm only leavin' presents
    Whar de chil'un mighty good."

Yo' kain't beleebe it, chil'un,
    But hit 's hones' as de day,
De monsus load ob presents
    Dat is piled up in dat sleigh.
Dar was little pony hosses, w'y,
    I gase dar was a million,
En little sleds, en dolls, en beds,
    Dar mus' a bin a billion;
En blocks, en games, en an'mul names,
    En monkey on a stick, en
'Nuff ob lasses kandy dar
    To make de hull worl' sick;

Santa's Presents fo' de Good

En little dogs en nanny goats—
    Ef yo' mus' heah me talk,
I saw a little bogie man
    Dat ac'chley could walk.

En ostriches, en singin' birds,
    A-standin' on a wiah;
En little hose cyart enjines, too,
    Fo' puttin' out a fiah,
En Noah en his an'muls,
    All gwine into de ark;
En devil feesh, en scuttle feesh.
    I jes' want yo' ter hark
About a little hoo-doo man
    Dat had a funny tail;
En den I saw a Jonah man
    A-swallerin' a whale.
Yo' nevah can imagine jes'
    What Santie could o' had,
En none at all fo' chil'un
    Dat is impident en bad;
But all dat go to school en learn,
    En try ter ach up good
Will sholy git a present,
    En he wants hit undahstood.

HEART OF HEARTS

OH, heart of hearts, how heartily thou beatest;
    Each tender beat beats all the rest. Thou greetest
Me each morn with ever-constant thumping—
'T is thou, dear heart of hearts, that keeps me humping.

Oh, brow of brows! By thy cold sweat I 'm browsing;
Each wipe I give thee gives the children housing;
The sturdy arm each day sets thee to sweating—
Both thee and heart get all the gets I 'm getting.

Oh, will of wills! Oh, wilt thou not or will'st
Thou push me on? With grand endeavor fill'st
Thou my soul, the while ambitions blasting
Shake out the deeds that shall be everlasting.

SYCAMORE

PECOOLIARITY of his bark,
    An' yit not only that,
We found 'im every mornin' on
    The front peazzer mat.
So Cenath got ter likin' 'im,
    'N' one day says ter me,
"I'm goin' ter call 'im Sycamore,
    He sticks so cluss," says she.

She used ter sic 'im on the tramps
    That come aroun' the place,
'N' book agents 'n' other scamps,
    He'd give 'em all a chase—
He scooted over fences, an'
    Aroun' the farm he'd run,
'N' then come back 'n' wag his tail
    'S if he'd bin havin' fun.

I never had ter sic 'im on
    Ter any livin' thing,

Sycamore

I 've seed that dog take arter birds,
    Yes, birds 'at 's on the wing,
'N' chase 'em 'bout a mild er so,
    Ter see 'f they would n't light;
Then he 'd sit down 'n' watch 'em till
    They flew clean out er sight.

The dangdest dog he was t' hunt,
    'N' had the keenes' scent;
One day he smell'd an animile,
    An' after him he went.
To'rds dark he come a-laggin' back,
    'N' any one could tell
That Sycamore had captured 'im,
    We knew it mighty well.

He pulled out every rooster's tail
    I had aroun' the coop,
'N' kept our yaller Thomas cat
    Hid underneath the stoop.
An' when a vehicle druv by
    He 'd skoot out thro' th' door
'N' sic 'em down the dusty road
    A half a mild er more.

He 'd lay behin' the hottest stove
    'N' bark out in his sleep,

Sycamore

'N' work his jints 'n' try ter run
    'S if he was chasin' sheep,
Till last he took a fit one day
    'N' stagger'd 'roun' the floor;
We thought one time he would n't live
    Ter sic 'em any more.

He had fun with a peddler onct,
    An' chased 'im 'round the well.
I wish as you 'd a just bin there
    An' heerd that feller yell:
"Git out! Git out! Call off yer dog!"
    He thought his jig was up.
Says I: "Do n't be afraid o' him,
    He 's nothin' more 'n a pup."

He used ter sic the thunder, too,
    An 't used ter give us pain
Ter see him set out in a storm
    'N' bark up at the rain.
He 'd shift his head t' one side
    When he 'd hear the thunder roar,
'N' then bark all the harder 'f I 'd say:
    "Sic 'em, Sycamore!"

He sict all of my neighbor's sheep,
    'N' did a pile o' harm;

Sycamore

He took my horses and my colts
    'N' raced 'm 'roun' the farm.
I jist can see him runnin' yit,
    His tail a-flyin' high,
But why it is we're mournin' now
    Is how he come ter die.

I sold 'im to a farmer 'cause
    He got so cross an' mean,
When one day long in harves' time
    He jumpt a thrash machine.
They said he give one little yelp—
    'N' then went up the spout.
Poor Sycamore got harvested,
    That's what we're sad about.

We mourn to think our dear old friend
    At last got "squeezed in wheat."
They found his collar—tail—some hair—
    The rest was sausage meat.
His gentle bark had sailed away
    Far to some canine shore.
My wife shed tears 'n' said, "Poor dog,
    He never 'll sic 'em more."

VOLAPUK

WHEN I can speak
      Volapuk,
Away to India's clime's I'll sneak,
And on my adamantine cheek
I'll sell a piano to a sheik.

I'll sell the French and Dutch,
      And lease
Pianos to the Portuguese;
Then I'll drive over and explain
The new installment plan to Spain.

I'll journey south as far
      As Cadiz,
And sell fair Andalusia's ladies
Or I'll exchange; the mandolin
I'll take, and put an upright in.

I'll hie me then
      To Baltic strand,
And sell Miss Boskovitch a grand;

Volapuk

And shovel off old Peter Katzski,
Romanoff and Ruffonratsky.

Then far to Greenland
    I will go,
And sell the sawed off Esquimaux;
I'll eat snow soup and Polar bear,
And try and work 'em on a square.

Of course by this time
    I'll have a
Cheek as hard as Hecla's lava;
I'll travel West, go through Alaska,
Drop down and talk with Mrs. Chaska.

I'll court the Fijis
    On their isle,
The old chief's daughter I'll beguile,
And talk piano by her side
While I am waiting to be fried,
    When I can speak
    Volapuk.

MARY HAD A CACTUS PLANT

MARY had a cactus plant,
    So modestly it grew,
Shooting its little fibers out
    It lived upon the dew.

Her little brother often heard
    Her say it lived on air,
And so he pulled it up one day
    And placed it in a chair.

Placed it in a chair he did,
    Then laughed with ghoulish glee—
Placed it in the old arm-chair
    Under the trysting tree.

Nor thought of Mary's lover,
    Who called each night to woo,
Or even dreamed they'd take a stroll,
    As lovers often do.

The eve drew on. The lover came,
    They sought the trysting tree.
Where has the little cactus gone?
    The lover—where is he?

THE DAY AND THE SHINGLE
(A PARODY.)

THE day is done and the spanker,
    So oft in the hands of mother,
Is soon to be wafted downward
    On little red-headed brother.

I can hear the fall of the shingle
    And poor little brother's refrain,
And a feeling of sadness comes o'er me
    That seems to resemble a pain.

A feeling of sadness and sorrow
    That must be akin to pain,
It resembles a seated sorrow
    That boyhood can only explain.

So I hie me away to the attic
    And put on a few pair of pants,
And wedge in a big paper bustle
    Belonging to one of my aunts.

The Day and the Shingle

I can see the lights of the village,
    And also the deep muddy pool,
Where often I ducked little brother
    After the close of school.

But she calls me down from the attic
    And asks me to take off my clothes,
With her able-bodied assistance
    I get myself ready to pose.

I take a recumbent position,
    The shingle then comes into play,
Johnnie sits down in a corner
    And watches the sad matinée.

As she presses her thin lips together
    I feel that at every rebound
She puts on a vermilion finish
    Where my back forms sort of a mound.

Such things have power to quiet
    The restless pulse of care,
But it makes it rather uneasy
    To sit on a hard-bottom chair.

Come read to me some poem,
    Some "Favorite Prescription" lay,

The Day and the Shingle

That will soothe this restless feeling
    And take the stinger away.

Read from some humbler poet
    A poem that relieves—
Something that's cold and frigid,
    From Wilcox or Amelie Rives.

And the kitchen shall cease its sobbing,
    And the cares that infest the day
Will quietly fold their breeches
    And silently steal away.

HUCCUM IT SO?

HUCCUM de cows so early home,
    Befo' de milkin' houah?
Bekase dey hyard it thundah, an'
    Knew las' night's milk was souah.

Huccum de she cat in de bahn,
    Up in de ole hay mow?
Bekase she 's intuhrested some
    In raisin' kittens now.

Huccum de darkes' hoss to win
    Dat great big derby race?
Bekase he had de stuff in him
    An' was n't held fo' place.

Huccum dat sobah bank casheah
    To pack his trunk and get?
Bekase he knew dat Montreal
    Laid ovah Joliet.

Huccum dat gal so shapely
    Dat fas'nates ebery lad?

Huccum It So

Bekase she 's got de sugah
    An' knows jes' how to pad.

Huccum dat han'some No'th Side girl
    To make de public scoff?
Bekase her uppah story it
    Was jes' a little off.

Huccums de eyarf a shakin' up
    An' scarin' people so?
Bekase dat 's jes' how Belzebub
    Remin's us ob below.

Huccums de trees a-glis'nin' an'
    De grass all wet wid dew?
Bekase why, chile, de atmosfeah
    Had nuffin' else to do.

Huccum dese metafizicks
    A-healin' people so?
Do n't ask me no mo' questions, chile,
    I tole yo' I do n't know.

DE WATAH MELLEN SPLOSHUN

DAR 'S one fing dat Hi would n't do
    Ef I had any common sense,
    Go sneakin' up to massa's fence
An' steal a watah mellen fro.
      Would you?

Hi kno' dat mos'ly fro de day
    He 's layin' out dar in de sun
    Behin' dat haystack wid a gun.
Hit 's loaded wid rock salt, an' say—
      You jay!

Do n't fool aroun' dem mellens dar,
    Torpeders grow dar 'pon dat vine;
    One busted las' night long 'bout nine,
An' lifted some po' niggah's har.
      See hyar—

Hi saw de sploshun when it 'cur'd;
    Hi saw dat coon a-flyin' hence

De Watah Mellen Sploshun

Off yondah ovah dat rail fence.
Of course, I would n't say a word.
   I hyard

Dat mos' de fahmers 'tach'd a line
   To mellens filled with dinahmite.
   Yo' coons dat's gwine out dar to-night
Jes' scuse me ; gase I 'll stay behin'.
   Now, min'!

You kno' Ole Birch, dat had one eye,
   Dat always got to church so soon,
   An' 'clar'd de eyarf went 'roun' de moon,
An' said dat jes' de reason why
   De sky

In night time needed bettah light,
   Was jes' 'cause wicked coons would steal
   From ebbery watah mellen fiel',
But Gord would burn 'em up some night.
   Dat's right.

He was n't to de church to-day ;
   A bran new coon stood in de spot
   An' set right whar he always sot.
He was n't dar to shout an' pray,
   Dat's what.

De Watah Mellen Sploshun

Hi doan s'pose none yo' niggahs hyard
    De reason dat I laft in church
    When some coon ast fo' Bruddah Birch.
'T was jes' las' night dat, 'pon my word,
    De sploshun 'cur'd.

No, sah! Hit 's neva gwine ter do
    Fo' any coon wid common sense
    To sneak up now to any fence
An' try to steal a mellen fro,
    Dat 's shuah.

MISS BAHTHOLAMEW

SPECKS we 's gwine to hab a time
'Bout dat free mile fishin' line.
    Dar 's a ring
    'Roun' de moon,
Sign dat trouble 's comin' soon.

We 's been layin' 'roun' so long,
Gettin' rich an' growin' strong ;
    Reckon 't won't
    Be much fun
Stoppin' balls dat weigh a ton.

Specks de vey fus' ting dey do,
Dey 'll shoot at Miss Bahtholamew ;
    Po' ole gal,
    Standin' dar,
Squintin' o'er de sea so far.

Ris up, den, ole Uncle Sam ;
Punch 'em wid a batterin' ram ;

Miss Bahtholamew

    Hit 'em lef,
    Hit 'em right,
Blow 'em up wid dinahmite.

Long as Miss Bahtholamew
Casts 'er shaddah on de blue,
    Let us stan',
    One an' all,
Waitin' fo' de kentry's call.

Hise de flag dat made us free
When de boys marched to de sea;
    Jine an' sing,
    Ebery man,
Hail Columby! Happy lan'.

Keep Miss Libahty in sight,
Holdin' out de mighty light;
    Gib free cheers,
    A tigah, too,
'Rah fo' Miss Bahtholamew!

THE COW SLIPS AWAY

THE tall pines pine,
    The pawpaws pause,
And the bumble-bee bumbles all day;
    The eavesdropper drops,
    And the grasshopper hops,
While gently the cow slips away.

THIS BOOK WAS PRINTED BY
R. R. DONNELLEY AND SONS
COMPANY AT THE LAKESIDE
PRESS, CHICAGO, FOR FORBES
AND COMPANY, PUBLISHERS.

www.ingramcontent.com/pod-product-compliance
Lightning Source LLC
Chambersburg PA
CBHW032054220426
43664CB00008B/996